DEVELOPING COLLECTIONS TO EMPOWER LEARNERS

ISBN: 978-0-8389-8728-5

Published by:
American Association of School Librarians
a division of the American Library Association
50 E. Huron St.
Chicago, Illinois 60611-2795

To order, call 800-545-2433, press 7
<www.alastore.ala.org/aasl>

Copyright ©2014 by the American Library Association. All rights reserved except those that may be granted by Sections 107 and 108 of the Copyright Revision Act of 1976. Printed in the United States of America.

Acknowledgments

AASL gratefully acknowledges the following:

Written by:
Sue C. Kimmel
Assistant Professor of Library Science
Department of Teaching and Learning
Old Dominion University, North Carolina
<skimmel@odu.edu>

AASL Staff Liaison: Stephanie Book

Purchases of AASL publications fund advocacy, leadership, professional development, and standards and guidelines initiatives for school librarians nationally.

Table of Contents

Introduction: *See Also*

Today's libraries are experiencing significant shifts brought on by increasingly digital and mobile technologies. I remember the hard physical work of literally shifting shelves in a library to make room for growth in the collection; the shift had to be strategic to meet both the very current need for space and to plan for the near future. It was hard work, and we didn't want to get to the end of the shelves and find we had miscalculated and still didn't have enough space.

The shift generally involved looking at crowded shelves in one section and shifting books to another less-crowded section, often around a corner, or, if we were really unlucky, on another floor. Resources were shifted based on careful calculations and planning. The best plans looked at the overall collection and determined where growth was occurring or weeding was needed. And they were considerate of the library patrons and how they would find materials. Even so, some patrons found the shift of physical resources difficult. Patrons had, for example, become accustomed to finding the dinosaur books on one particular shelf.

I see similar characteristics in today's shifts toward digital resources. What kinds of physical shifts may occur on our school library shelves as, for example, less space is needed for reference books or bound journals? How will we let our patrons know that materials have shifted—especially now that the new location is virtual?

Today's shifts toward new formats and devices are unsettling for many librarians, who wonder, "What do these shifts mean for us and our patrons. We even hear dire predictions about the demise of libraries as people find information accessible literally at their fingertips. But I believe that even as we feel the sands shifting beneath our feet, we stand on a firm foundation of our profession's commitment to quality resources and service, access, and a learning society. We may be shifting shelves, but we still have the big picture and the foundational needs of our patrons in mind. Librarians select, organize, and provide access to resources. They apply their professional expertise to meet the needs of their local community.

I have been a patron of libraries all of my life. One of the more important discoveries I made in the library card catalog was the "See Also" reference. These references were a kind of hypertext that suggested a jump from the original search query into a related field. In this introduction I will use the See Also reference to jump through some of the key moments that have brought me to the authorship of this book.

AUTHOR *SEE ALSO* CHAIR OF AASL TASK FORCE ON QUANTITATIVE STANDARDS

I was the chair of a task force charged with examining whether AASL should consider new national quantitative standards for school library collections. In that process, the task force explored the history of quantitative standards in various kinds of libraries as well as state efforts to implement them for school libraries.

We also considered what the research said about the shortcomings of such quantitative measures and the need for a professional librarian to interpret and apply them. An interesting finding was a shift in language. A search for "standards" in *Library Literature and Information Science* over the past decade was more likely to result in learning standards.

Finally, we wondered how to meaningfully count new digital formats and the devices needed to access them. The measures that seemed most meaningful today were about student learning and about student access to the resources they needed for learning. We provided our report to AASL and were invited to construct a position statement for AASL on Quantitative Standards (see Appendix E). The idea for a book on collection development for school libraries that was inclusive of new and shifting formats grew out of this work.

CHAIR OF TASK FORCE *SEE ALSO* SCHOOL LIBRARIAN

Today I teach pre-service school librarians at a university. For almost twenty years I worked in school libraries, first as an assistant and then as a school librarian. Much of this book is based on my own experiences working in four different schools with a total of seven different principals who provided varying degrees of support for the library program and its budget. Those experiences included opening a new school and selecting the entire opening-day collection. Throughout this book I draw on these experiences, including the history I witnessed in the transformation of school library collections. I remember card catalogs, phonograph records, and sound filmstrips, personal computers—primitive by today's standards—and modems. I also remember the value of a library advisory committee and actively building support with principals and parent-teacher associations. And I remember the thrill of placing the right book in the hands of the right child at the right time.

SCHOOL LIBRARIAN *SEE ALSO* BOOK REVIEWER

Concurrent with being a school librarian I was also fortunate to work as a book reviewer. My favorite professional development involved meeting with colleagues to discuss new resources and their relationship to curriculum standards. These discussions were a delightful way to expand my understanding of both curriculum and evaluating media. I also served on the Association for Library Service to Children's Caldecott, Newbery, and Notable Books for Children committees; these experiences sharpened my understandings of selection criteria applied to different genres and forms. My start in reviewing was as a selector for Brodart's *Elementary School Library Collection*, a biennial selection tool that was published as a book and CD-ROM.

BOOK REVIEWER *SEE ALSO* BIBLIOGRAPHER

My first professional library job was not in a library; I was the bibliographer for *Elementary School Library Collection (ESLC)*, working in the editorial offices for this publication. With the authorship of *Developing Collections to Empower Learners*, I feel like I have come back full circle to this experience. *ESLC* had a collection-level perspective on school library selection. Selectors applied selection criteria that included value to the collection including comparing new materials against existing recommendations for coverage, currency, and quality.

Materials in all formats, not just print books, were considered. One of my tasks as the bibliographer was to create combined entries of books and other media based on a book. This experience first showed me how books morphed into filmstrips, audiobooks, videos, and even interactive software or "talking books." *ESLC* was a collection described in a book, and my work on *ESLC* taught me to see collections as interlocking, interdependent, fluid, and shifting. I also learned to appreciate the work and thought that go into an authoritative library-selection tool, and the value of that work to practicing librarians who select for readers.

BIBLIOGRAPHER *SEE ALSO* READER

Okay, I'll confess. One of the perks of being the bibliographer for *ESLC* was getting to view and even read many of the books that came across my desk. I have always been a reader, and without libraries I could never satisfy my appetite for books. Today I am omnivorous in my reading habits. I read print books, magazines, and newspapers. I spend hours every day reading online resources, including blogs and journal articles that have also informed the writing of this book. I read e-books and magazines and enjoy the ease of access they provide. Throughout this book I am talking as a school library professional, but I am also conscious of myself as a reader, a library patron, and a lifelong learner. This book was written with young people in mind—both the ones who come into our libraries today and the ones who don't…yet. How do we build and shift our collections to meet their needs and interests?

Chapter 1

Who Are We?

Close your eyes and envision a library. Does it contain shelves of books in a myriad of colors and sizes standing in orderly lines? Do the books entice you with their promises of new facts, new characters, new places, and new ideas? Do you long to sit in carpeted aisles, read the spines, reach for volumes, and turn their pages?

If you are a school librarian, perhaps these are the warm, fuzzy memories you have of your own childhood among the stacks in a school or public library. But as a school librarian today you have another vision of the school library as a space filled with eager students interacting with books, computers, cell phones, and other people. Teachers breeze in to quickly collaborate with the librarian. Students stop by to return or check out materials. Facts, characters, places, and ideas circulate in this space and through a variety of channels. The shelves are unruly; their contents shift shape, size, and space. Books don't always live on shelves, and some move from library catalog to individual devices without ever taking physical form or needing space on the shelves. This scenario also entices us with its endless energy, possibilities, and promises.

We occupy spaces today with shifting shelves, and it's exciting but also a bit unsettling. We used to be defined by our collections, and they had a heft and presence that demanded our attention and our time. Even when our libraries were empty of students and teachers, our collections provided seeming evidence of the importance of our work. We tended those collections, shelved new materials, and re-shelved returned materials and stray books. Everything had a place, and the place was carefully tended. We measured our effectiveness by counting volumes, calculating volumes per student, determining the collection's age, and noting numbers of titles added, titles weeded, circulations of volumes, and even feet of shelving. We presented these numbers as measures of our worth. Yet the mission of school libraries "to ensure that students and staff are effective users of ideas and information" (AASL 2009, 8) demands a different kind of accounting: one focused on users, and one that is best attained through unruly shelves that shape-shift to meet the needs and interests of those users.

When scanning the titles of school library standards (see table 1), it's easy to see other shifts in our history, including what must have been a major upheaval in 1969, when the terminology shifted from "school libraries" to "school media programs." The terminology changed to be more inclusive of multiple formats for information and ideas. Subsequent decades saw filmstrips shift to videocassettes, and then to DVDs and streaming online video. Similar shifts occurred in audio and other formats.

Through each of these shifts, school librarians rushed to acquire the new media to ensure up-to-date access to ideas and information, and invested in new equipment to ensure effective use of each new medium. Often these new formats were expensive or required special equipment to access; perceptions of scarcity or concern about loss led to placing multimedia formats on segregated teacher-only shelves. Each of these shifts required new uses of library spaces to accommodate shelving and access to new types of resources.

"RADICAL CHANGE" IN BOOKS

Book collections were often the primary media available for direct student access even as prices dropped on multimedia formats and home equipment became more ubiquitous. Book collections were not immune to transforma-

Table 1. Shifts in professional terminology throughout the decades.

Selected Guidelines and Standards	
1918	Standard Library Organization and Equipment for Secondary Schools of Different Sizes
1925	Elementary School Library Standards
1945	School Library Standards for Today and Tomorrow
1969	Standards for School Media Programs
1988	Information Power: Guidelines for School Library Media Programs
2009	Empowering Learners: Guidelines for School Library Programs

Source: "A History of School Library Media Program Standards and Guidelines" in *Empowering Learners* (AASL 2009, 55–56).

tions, undergoing what Eliza Dresang has characterized as a "radical change" as their pages became more visual, non-linear, and interactive, and the content became more unsettled including topics and points of view previously neglected in children's literature. Dresang defines this radical change as changing forms and formats, changing perspectives, and changing boundaries in what she terms "handheld books" (Dresang 1999, 17). Books, according to Dresang, were changing to reflect the needs and interests of young readers who expected connectivity, interactivity, and easy access to information (Dresang 1999, 12–13). She provides numerous examples, including the *Magic School Bus* series, which integrated a fictional story line with a graphic format and bites of information.

The Magic School Bus was difficult for librarians to classify because of its mix of fantasy and fact. Did school librarians decide to classify it for placement on the fiction shelves arranged by author or with nonfiction according to subject? When the first book in the series, *The Magic School Bus at the Waterworks,* was released, librarians debated where to place the book. Some collections may still have it in the fiction section. When graphic novels appeared, many librarians shifted their collections to shelve graphic novels by format in the 700s, and this section of the shelves burgeoned. Library collections have always been unruly, and librarians are familiar with having to shift shelves to make space for growth in the collection—especially when some areas grow more than others. Change should be a familiar aspect of our jobs.

SHIFTS TO ELECTRONIC FORMATS

Currently we are in an unsettled time as resources morph into more fluid electronic formats. School libraries have noted this shift already in terms of periodical and reference collections. Various printed encyclopedias, and periodical indexes and sources have moved into digital formats that allow more flexibility and more access points. Digital resources require a shift in dollars, and have often led to shared purchasing of periodical databases and online reference tools by a school district or state library. When the first electronic multimedia encyclopedias were introduced, they provided the kinds of access print never offered: multiple simultaneous users; continuous updates; links to video, images, maps, and audio clips; and enhanced search capability. Print encyclopedias, on the other hand, were expensive and took up a lot of shelf space. Each volume of an encyclopedia could be used by only one user at a time, and circulations were limited. With the onset of electronic encyclopedias, libraries were faced with decisions about whether to continue to purchase the print version; at first, many maintained both. Some eliminated or reduced the frequency and number of purchases of print encyclopedias, thereby freeing up shelf space and some funding that could be diverted to more-specialized materials.

Periodical collections have also shifted with the availability of online databases. Libraries no longer subscribe to print magazine indexes or retain many past issues of periodicals. As print magazine collections were needed less for research, libraries focused acquisitions on reader interests and allowed issues to circulate. E-books will offer similar challenges and diversions of funds, as well as similar opportunities for increased access, freeing of space, and collections focused on appeal to the user for pleasure (like the periodical collection) and for specialized kinds of resources (like the reference collection). School systems and schools may look for ways to share purchasing and access to e-books to increase access and lower or maintain costs, just as the cost of many database subscriptions have been shared.

QUESTIONS ABOUT NEW SHIFTS

These shifts to electronic formats continue to raise questions about our print collections. Some predict the demise of nonfiction as it goes the way of reference. Why check out an entire book when only one chapter is needed? Will fiction and nonfiction shift to serve recreational reading, going the way of many magazine collections? What parts of the collection still work best in print? What user needs are best served by print? What about access issues for students with disabilities or those learning a new language?

As space becomes available, how might we use that space in new ways? Is there room to collect and disseminate new kinds of resources? Will we have more space for collaborative work? What kinds of spaces and tools should we offer for media production? Should we extend to more users the types of tools we provide? What devices should we provide: more desktop computers, laptops, tablets, e-readers? And what about the types of infrastructure needed to sustain access to those devices, such as charging stations, power cords, and synching stations? In the past, school libraries kept the equipment locked up. Is it time to give students more access? Some school libraries have darkrooms, video-editing equipment, and sound rooms for recording broadcasts. How should these now be used to join the stream of media creation and dissemination by students?

A driving force in today's information and media landscape is the burgeoning availability of Web resources via the Internet. When students now have access to so much more content than our libraries could physically hold, what should our libraries look like? What should our role be in selecting and developing collections for user access to online resources? What does a library do now that people can get the books and information they want on demand? Now even mass media can be tailored to user interests including the music a person prefers, the news the person agrees with, the weather for the local zip code, and customized suggestions ("if you like this book or movie, you might like these others").

LIBRARY AS MEDIATION

One way to think of our mission "to ensure that students and staff are effective users of ideas and information" (AASL 2009, 8) is to see ourselves as mediators who—with each small decision we make about what to collect and how to provide access to each item in our collection—actively provide a layer between those users and the wide world of "ideas and information." How often have we heard someone talk about the value of browsing the library shelves and the patron's sense of serendipity in unexpectedly finding exactly the item that was needed? This sense of serendipity and discovery was provided through the mediation of a librarian who anticipated that need, selected that item, and made a calculated decision about how to catalog and where to shelve it to maximize the possibility that it would be discovered. Lester Asheim said about selection: "it is here that we exert, however indirectly, our greatest influence on the public we serve and the total society of which the public is a part" (1979, 9–10). Decisions about selection determine what is accessible to library patrons, and nobody, Asheim argued, was better qualified to make those decisions than the librarian. Today, we are faced with new formats and virtual shelves, but this key aspect of our profession, to mediate access for our users through the selection and development of library collections, remains as critical as ever.

As Asheim noted, what sets us apart from the mass media is that we do not broadcast to everyone; we serve the multiple needs of our multiple users (1979, 13). The library continues to serve a different purpose than other media outlets. We have a long tradition of using predetermined criteria to select, without bias, the best resources for our users. We aren't trying to sell a product or a particular point of view. In school libraries it's particularly important to offer a broad selection of resources to the young people we serve as they form tastes and opinions. As young people are in the process of trying on new identities, too much customization might have the effect of prematurely foreclosing other possibilities. Libraries, especially school libraries, have an important role to play through the selection of the best from a variety of genres, multiple perspectives, and appropriate formats.

The selection of the best resources from the universe of possible resources has always been a form of mediation provided by librarians. Today, when the amount of available information is growing more rapidly every year, this form of mediation is needed more than ever.

ACCESS

School libraries are about access. As some things shift and have always shifted, this fundamental role of supporting the educational mission of a school through access to necessary resources will continue to serve as a key role.

Print collections provided accessibility through the physical presence of the books selected, cataloged, and shelved in our libraries. Today, if we continue to think of our collections in terms of what our patrons can access, what should our collection-development plans look like? Increasingly, the most important element is not what we own, but what we subscribe to, connect to, or the networks we belong to.

In this shifting scenario, the school library and school librarian continue to serve an important intermediary function between the user, and ideas and information. The resources we select may be databases, websites, or memberships in consortia that share e-books and other types of resources and expertise. The school library becomes a filter in the most positive sense of the word as a conduit between the needs of the school community and the wide world of possible resources.

EMPOWERING LEARNERS

Information Power, program guidelines developed in 1998 by AASL and the Association for Educational Communications and Technology, marked a shift to school librarians as instructional partners with a role in teaching that included student standards for information literacy. AASL's *Empowering Learners: Guidelines for School Library Programs* (2009) followed publication of AASL's *Standards for the 21st-Century Learner* (2007) and represented yet another shift from consumption to creation. *Empowering Learners* was framed within the context of the revised mission of the school library program and included more-specific language outlining how the school librarian "empowers students to be critical thinkers, enthusiastic readers, skillful researchers, and ethical users of information" (AASL 2009, 8).

A copy of the revised and extended mission statement is included in the Appendix E. The school librarian in this mission statement is charged not only with "providing access to materials in all formats" but with instructing and assisting students and staff in "using, evaluating, and producing information and ideas." "Effective" use has been broadened to promote this "active" engagement with information and ideas. To fulfill this mission the school librarian is expected to have knowledge of "a broad range of appropriate tools, resources, and information technologies," "up-to-date, high-quality, varied literature," and anticipate "changes in technology and education" (AASL 2009, 8). Our knowledge, in other words, needs to be broad, up-to-date, and responsive to change.

Our focus should always be on learners and their effective actions in this shifting landscape. Our actions—and learners'—are no longer just about consumption, but about knowledge creation. School libraries are also becoming creation spaces where effective users of ideas and information find the tools needed to create and share their own knowledge productions (see figure 1).

WE ARE LIBRARIANS

Empowering Learners offers significant guidance for developing collections and advocating for "the creation of a collection development plan that uses virtual and physical resources wisely" (AASL 2009, 39) and provides both flexibility and a forward-looking vision to allow consideration of these emerging questions. Each of the roles of school librarian as described in *Empowering Learners*—leader, instructional partner, information specialist, teacher, and program administrator—cannot be separated from the fundamental, social, and historical value of libraries as spaces and collections mediated by the judgment and selection skills of a professional librarian (see figure 2). Our primary focus and responsibility expressed in *Empowering Learners* and *Standards for the 21st-Century Learner* is to the learner. We understand the types of

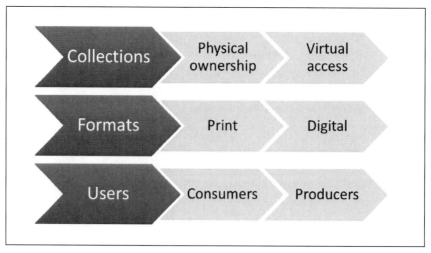

Figure 1. Key shifts influencing today's school libraries.

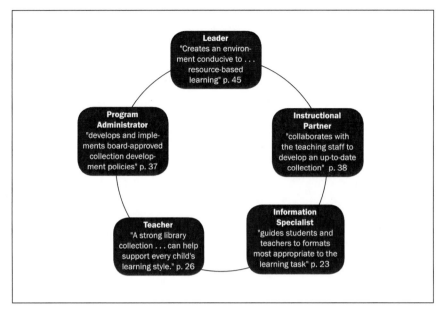

Figure 2. Collection development integrated with the five roles of the school librarian from *Empowering Learners.*

decisions needed to ensure 21st-century learners have access to the resources needed to be effective consumers and producers of information and ideas heading into the twenty-second century. We are librarians.

The chapters of this book will address issues of collection development as related to two major shifts: toward increasingly digital resources and access, and toward users as both consumers and creators of content.

Collection development is anchored in the cultural and historical roles of libraries as providing a community of users with access to information and ideas. Several fundamental principles, including needs assessment, selection, budgeting, acquisition tasks, and a cycle of planning and evaluation are as relevant as ever.

This book will also focus on new formats, issues of ownership and devices, and questions about "what counts" in collection-development plans. Additionally, the growing interest in school libraries as centers for student production will be addressed both in terms of acquisitions and the curation of those products.

REFLECTIVE QUESTIONS

▶ What will being an "effective user of ideas and information" mean in five, ten, or twenty years?

▶ What types of tools should school librarians select and collect for patrons?

▶ Does it make sense to limit access to parts of a collection for specific groups of users?

▶ How might we create opportunities for user serendipity in virtual collections?

▶ How is the knowledge and selection of quality resources implied in each of the roles of school librarian as described in *Empowering Learners:* leader, instructional partner, information specialist, teacher, and program administrator?

Chapter 2

What Is Collection Development?

ITERATIVE PROCESS

Collection development is the ongoing process of identifying needs and then selecting, managing, and evaluating a collection of materials to meet those needs. It's a cyclical process with an evaluation of existing conditions leading to the identification of gaps or needs and so on (see figure 3). Driving each phase of the cycle is the learning mission of the school and the needs of learners.

Collection development is a very deliberate process that intersects with each of the five roles of the school librarian outlined in *Empowering Learners*. In the process of collection development, the school librarian deliberately draws on each of these roles—leader, instructional partner, information specialist, teacher, and program administrator—to understand how a carefully selected and organized collection of resources can support the big-picture mission of the school as well as the very particular needs of members of the school community. Careful attention to these needs, in turn, informs the development of that collection. Each role is fueled

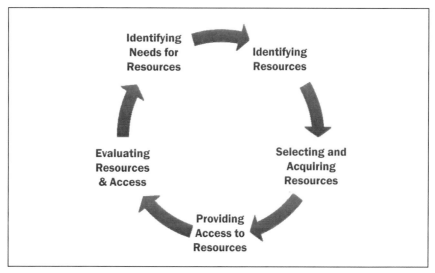

Figure 3. Collection-development continuous-improvement cycle.

by an awareness of available resources. Development of the collection is an organic process responsive to the evolving needs of learners and the school's mission. Leaders leverage this process to maximize the value and diffusion of the collection for all members of the learning community.

While this is a book about collection development, readers should find application to many other aspects of the job of school librarian. The purpose of the school library collection should be so deeply embedded in the learning mission of the school that developing the collection in isolation would be meaningless. Much of the ideas in this book about knowing students, their families, and communities, and thinking about how best to meet learners' needs for information, reading, and communication are just ideas about good librarianship, good teaching, good leadership, and good management.

Collection development is about having a plan. *Empowering Learners* offers significant advice about planning for the school library program that can be translated into planning for the collection. *A Planning Guide for Empowering Learners* (2010) provides guidance and a rubric for evaluating a school library program by means of a process that includes input from various stakeholders. A collection-development plan that emerges from this planning process would include long-term strategic planning that reflects the school's mission, goals, and objectives. Data should be collected and analyzed from an ongoing evaluation not only of the collection but also of the learning outcomes and needs of students as those factors impact the collection. A collection-development plan should also include guiding statements about access, intellectual freedom, and equity.

WHY COLLECTION DEVELOPMENT REQUIRES A PLAN

A collection-development plan focuses on the big picture and situates the collection within the larger goals of the school. A big-picture plan provides justification for the resources—money, time, and space—needed not to support the collection but to support the mission, goals, and objectives of the school. A collection-development plan clearly illustrates how the collection is a means, not an end. The school library's collection of resources is an important means to support the delivery of the school's curriculum and to support the informational needs and recreational interests of students.

Unless this focus is clearly articulated, it's easy for stakeholders, including the librarian, to see the development of a collection as an end in itself. The point is not to have an up-to-date collection with all the materials anyone would ever want. Instead, the point is to have a collection that meets the needs of students and staff in a specific school for up-to-date, accessible, relevant, high-quality materials so that the school's curriculum goals can be reached. A collection-development plan communicates this focus to all stakeholders.

Collection development cannot be accomplished without a plan. Without a plan the addition of new materials, new formats, or new devices to the collection is subject to the whims of individuals, current fads, and clever sales pitches. Developing a collection is not simply a matter of adding new items. Development is a very deliberate process. Every item is carefully selected to fill an identified need.

WHAT'S IN THE COLLECTION-DEVELOPMENT PLAN

A collection-development plan provides a big-picture view of the collection. In any given year, updating every part of the collection may not be possible. In some years the roll-out of a new format or a new curriculum may require an infusion of attention and resources to one aspect of the collection. A long-range plan ensures that other areas of the collection are also considered and will receive more attention in subsequent years. One strategy is to divide the collection into thirds and plan to address each third of the collection in depth every three years.

Developers of a collection-development plan consider and articulate the strengths and weaknesses for each segment of the collection. Just as the entire collection is reflected in the plan, all stakeholders should also see themselves in the plan. One way to ensure inclusion is to include representation from all stakeholders in the development and dissemination of the plan.

Issues related to the addition of resources, including where they will be shelved or housed, how they will be accessed, and any special equipment or other processing needed for access, should also be considered. Questions of access should include consideration of the need for multiple copies or multiple formats for the content. Who might need this content and what types of access will they need?

A collection-development plan will also include action steps, a timeline, and budget projections. Students' learning outcomes should drive each step in the process to emphasize the collection as a means, not an end. As a leader in the school, the school librarian should seek input from all stakeholders into the plan including teachers, students, and parents. A written document that projects three to five years into the future with annual benchmarks will help to guide current as well as future decisions and serve as a blueprint for the continuous improvement of the collection.

At the same time, it's important to recognize the fluid nature of technology, formats, and devices. A long-term plan should allow for flexibility but also provide cause to consider the long-range ramifications of current decisions. Can a decision to purchase a particular e-reading device be sustained for several years? This decision must also be balanced by the fact that most of our students matriculate through a school within a three- to five-year term. A decision not to purchase a particular format or device may deny many students access to that particular technology.

Collection-development plans that employ tools such as Google Docs or a wiki allow for updating and sharing the plan. Online tools such as these enable direct links to the district selection policy and other supporting documents. Additionally, an online collection-development plan could be widely disseminated through a link from the school's or school library's website or by sharing the URL through newsletters and other venues.

OVERVIEW OF THE REMAINING CHAPTERS

The chapters of this book are arranged to lead the reader through the various steps of the collection-development cycle and planning with a particular focus on the new landscape of digital resources. The purpose of each chapter is to lead the reader through a consideration of what must be included in a "wise collection-development plan" as promoted in *Empowering Learners.*

Chapter three focuses on a needs assessment as the first step in a collection-development plan. Needs are identified through formal and informal assessments. Such assessments include thinking about the library's clientele: Who are they now and who will they be in the future? Authors of an effective collection-development plan look forward, and consider current and future needs. Given that the instructional needs of students and teachers are largely determined by the curriculum, a needs assessment will attend to local, state, and national standards. Standards may themselves be under a schedule of regular revision. A collection plan will also include plans for continuous assessments. As all patrons are considered in a collection-development plan, in a needs assessment careful attention is also given to issues of equity related to access.

Chapters four through six examine collection development in today's rapidly changing information landscape through three scenarios. In these chapters the focus will be on thinking about different formats, including, but not limited to, print books. Today's collection-development plans cannot ignore the proliferation of new formats, and the wise decisions that must be made in their selection and in providing access to all students and staff. These chapters widen the focus to include not only the kinds of physical formats that form a collection but other kinds of collections such as digital curations, locally generated materials, and tools. School librarians have always had to think about containers for items: books needed jackets, DVDs required protective cases, and book and tape kits needed hanging bags. Today's formats raise similar questions about how to contain, provide access, and disseminate items.

Chapter seven deals explicitly with another question that is emerging as part of this new landscape: acquisitions of e-books and devices. Traditionally, libraries purchased items and added them to their collections. A library owned an item and loaned it to patrons. Increasingly, the items we purchase are digital, and our patrons access them online and require devices for access. Libraries subscribe to e-resources or license access, and might share access with other libraries or consortia. Other models are emerging, including patron-driven acquisitions. The wise use of library resources and the costs and benefits of these models must be weighed. A long-range perspective provided by a collection-development plan will help to guide librarians making these decisions and considering their short- and long-term ramifications.

Chapter eight looks in greater detail at the continuous evaluation of our collections. This chapter is a complement to the needs assessment discussed in chapter 3 but is particularly concerned with questions about how to quantify and otherwise document the library collection's value to the learning community. This chapter discusses evidence-based measures for demonstrating how the collection supports the educational mission of the school. As formats become more liquid, access more virtual, how do we make their value visible? In this chapter we will go beyond the traditional means of counting the number of items or number of circulations to more meaningful measures of value. The chapter takes a particular look at using this part of the collection-development plan to support advocacy efforts at the building, district, state, and national levels.

Chapter nine pulls back again to look at the big picture of collection development and provides action steps for readers to follow in creating their own collection-development plans and implementing them.

Each chapter will also include several reflective questions to guide readers through thinking about collection development. These questions will invite both students and practitioners to probe deeper about the kinds of issues that collection development raises as they relate to the school library profession and education of librarians and our students. Readers are invited to think about other documents that represent school libraries, all libraries, and education, and practitioners will be invited to share these probes with other stakeholders as they develop collection-development plans.

APPLICATIONS TO SCHOOL LIBRARY SETTINGS: THREE SCENARIOS

While this is a book about school library collections and about changing library formats, at heart it is a book that expresses an abiding belief in the importance of school libraries and the day-to-day work of school librarians in schools to promote learning, advocate for learners, and provide spaces for the enjoyment of inquiry and reading. In the following three scenarios, three school librarians are each wrestling with particular problems in today's shifting landscapes. In each of the remaining chapters, their settings will provide an opportunity to think about different aspects of collection development as applied in real settings.

Clarke Elementary School: Opening a New School

Sarah is excited that as the librarian, she will be a part of opening a new school, Clarke Elementary School, next fall. Her new principal has recognized the importance of the library and librarian to the new school, and Sarah is among the first of his hires for the new staff. The new elementary school will draw from three previous schools. She is responsible for the seemingly daunting task of selecting the opening collection for the school. Several vendors have contacted her about their "Opening Day" collections, but Sarah decides that she needs to be more intentional in her choice.

The questions that Sarah should consider as she builds a new collection from the ground up will allow us to think about the fundamentals of building a school library collection, starting with what we know about the school's community and teaching staff.

Champion High School: Responding to Changing Needs of Students

John is the school librarian at Champion High School, an anchor in the community for over seventy-five years. When he arrived eight years ago, he weeded the collection extensively. Since then, he has had a healthy budget, and now has a print collection that rivals the public library. In the past few years, however, he has seen the print reference collection used less and less as students and faculty prefer the Web, and students and parents have been pushing for electronic books.

Recently, the school has implemented a Bring Your Own Device (BYOD) policy, and students are using their devices to access the school's wireless network for research. John is faced with deciding how much of the collection to move to electronic format and how to maintain a balance with the print collection.

The scenario at Champion High School will allow us to consider how best to integrate new formats in a way responsive to student needs and interests as well as the struggle for a traditional library to remain relevant.

Einstein Middle School: A Space for Collaboration and Creation

Jean is the school librarian at Einstein Middle School. She has a dynamic program and collaborates regularly with teams of teachers. However, she has found herself focusing more and more on helping other educators in her school and her students take advantage of resources outside the library's walls. For example, she is creating just-in-time how-to videos and posting them on the school's network, leading students and staff to databases and websites she has curated. A large video collection (VHS tapes) is gathering dust, and the reference section has gotten smaller and smaller every year.

She recognizes an opportunity to capitalize on some space and decides to move into creating a "makerspace." She decides to pitch the plan to her library advisory committee using AASL's *Standards for the 21st-Century Learner* and finding correlations through AASL's Common Core State Standards Crosswalk <www.ala.org/aasl/standards-guidelines/crosswalk> to make the argument that students need to become producers not just consumers of information. Her team decides they should apply for a local grant as part of an ambitious plan to acquire tools for students to use to create audio, video, and games.

Einstein Middle School allows us to consider new possibilities for library collections and spaces. Jean will draw heavily on the implications for school libraries of the *Standards for the 21st-Century Learner* and school librarians' role in the academic mission of schools.

REFLECTIVE QUESTIONS

▶ Who are the stakeholders I need to consider for my collection-development plan?

▶ What documents do I currently have that represent or relate to a collection-development plan?

▶ What current issues related to the school library collection (curriculum, technology, school demographics, equity, etc.) are most pressing?

▶ How does the library collection impact collaboration with teachers?

Chapter 3

Attending to Gaps: Needs Assessment

WHERE TO BEGIN?

In her interview with the principal for the new school, Sarah is asked how she would start to identify and select the materials to order for the Clarke Elementary School's new library. Sarah begins by talking about what is known about the projected student enrollment, the communities they belong to, as well as the curriculum and the teaching staff. She asks the principal detailed questions about the projected characteristics of the students, including ethnicity, language, and socioeconomics. She also asks about data regarding the students' achievement levels and differentiated learning needs. Sarah uses the interview as an opportunity to collect information for the beginning of a needs assessment that, along with her knowledge of the elementary school curriculum, will assist her in making decisions about the collection. The principal is impressed with her focus on the learner, and Sarah gets the job.

WHAT IS A NEEDS ASSESSMENT?

A needs assessment is about identifying gaps between a desired state and an actual state (Kaufman

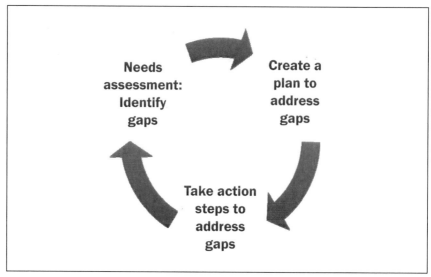

Figure 4. Needs assessment: a type of action research (Klobas 1997).

and English 1979). When applied to the library collection, the process is a matter of identifying gaps between the current collection and the ideal collection. An opening collection, like the one at Clarke Elementary School, would be a special case because no current collection exists. In this case, the ideal collection should be envisioned and resources expended toward achieving the vision. In all cases, limited budgets may require a wise distribution of funds toward the achievement of long-term goals.

A needs assessment helps to inform action steps that will move the collection toward the ideal vision. In this sense, a needs assessment is similar to the stages of action research described by Jane E. Klobas as "planning, action, and evaluation" (1997, 2) in that a problem is identified (the gap); action steps are developed and then implemented; the outcomes are assessed; and the cycle is reiterated with further steps. In collection development, we identify gaps in the collection, identify resources to fill the gaps, make a plan to acquire those resources, acquire the resources, measure their impact, and then make further plans. An ongoing collection of data for a needs assessment is a critical step in developing a collection.

What are the types of things we should consider in a needs assessment addressing a library collection? The school library collection serves the mission, goals, and objectives of the school, the school system, and the state. Our first consideration should be our learners—both present and future. The clientele of the school library and the curricula should inform identification of the ideal collection. Curricula, including local, state, and national standards, are important considerations. Identifying gaps also requires knowledge of the current collection. A needs assessment, therefore, develops a vision of the ideal collection needed to meet the needs of students and the mission of the school, and then measures this ideal against data about the current collection.

DIVERSITY OF STUDENT NEEDS

Empowering Learners frequently addresses the diversity of learners in terms of "gender, ethnicity, age, reading abilities and information needs" (AASL 2009, 38). *Empowering Learners* also references other kinds of diversity such as linguistic skills, disability, developmental and maturity levels, and learning styles. Much of this type of information can be found in school data about the demographics of the student body. School systems often engage in projections about future demographics as well, and this data can help to inform the long-range goals of the library's collection. Achievement data is often reported in aggregate but will likely include a breakdown by any existing subgroups, including gender, ethnicity, free- and reduced-lunch status, and disability. Free- and reduced-lunch status reports the percentage of students who receive assistance for food and is the measure of poverty most often available and used by schools. The school librarian who serves on leadership and other school-wide teams may have particular access to these kinds of data and will also be alert to the school's concern with particular achievement gaps. These types of data about the characteristics of the student population can also inform specific areas of the collection. And to the extent that the collection-development plan aligns with school improvement goals, requests for budgets can also align with these areas.

Several kinds of diversity are listed below. These may have different implications for the collection. On the one hand, the collection should reflect the racial and ethnic diversity of the community served by the school library; however, students should also see other racial and ethnic groups in the collection. Linguistic diversity might suggest the need for materials in other languages. Categories may interact in significant ways. For example, a stark difference in reading ability between genders may need to be addressed through the collection.

COMMUNITY AND NEIGHBORHOOD

To maximize the value of a needs assessment, a school librarian goes beyond the school's current data to look at the community and neighborhood (see table 2). For example, employment patterns, mobility, and issues related to socioeconomic levels may characterize the school's neighborhood and have an impact on future enrollments. School librarians have an overriding concern with equitable access to ideas and information. In today's technological landscape, this concern with equity should include an understanding of the kinds of access learners have outside of school to the technology needed to use information in digital and other formats. A needs assessment would identify these gaps and work to supply devices or extend library hours beyond the school day to ameliorate the effects of these gaps.

SCHOOL MISSION AND GOALS

The school library exists to support the mission and goals of the school. As part of a needs assessment, it's wise to know the mission and goals of the

Table 2. Types of student diversity.

Types of Student Diversity
race
ethnicity
gender
age
disability
linguistic skill level
religion
sexual orientation
socioeconomic status
reading ability
family structures
mobility
family employment

school and to direct plans for library resources toward the beliefs and priorities expressed in these established documents (see table 3). Generally, these address student achievement but frequently also include language about citizenship, dispositions, or character.

These lofty goals can also be addressed through the library's collection-development plan. As often as possible, the school librarian should attend leadership meetings, professional development sessions for teachers, school board meetings, parent-teacher association board meetings, and other departmental or grade-level meetings. Specific needs of the school are generally raised in these spaces and can inform library planning.

The school librarian who collaborates with teachers is positioned to understand the curriculum or standards as they are delivered and taught in specific classrooms by specific teachers. This understanding will often lead to the identification of gaps in the school library's collection.

STATE AND NATIONAL CONTENT STANDARDS

State and national standards guide what is taught and should also guide collection development. For example, if standards dictate that information about insects be taught in second grade, the school librarian knows that the library must contain books on insects that can be read and enjoyed by second-graders.

Table 3. Types of documents important to a needs assessment.

Types of Documents
mission statements
school-improvement plans
school data
attendance zone maps
minutes (e.g., of board meetings)
census reports
local newspapers
neighborhood blogs
state standards
national standards (e.g., NCTM)
Common Core State Standards
Standards for the 21st-Century Learner

This is the very specific kind of information that can guide selection.

Textbook adoptions and local interpretations of standards are also key determinants of how teachers will teach and the kinds of resources needed to support and extend learning. Most states regularly revisit and revise standards, and follow regular schedules for new textbook adoptions. School librarians should be attuned to these patterns and their potential impact on classroom practices and resource needs.

DEMANDS OF NEW STANDARDS

Champion High School's print collection has been well supported and well tended throughout the years. John attends leadership and PTA meetings, and prides himself on being attentive to community needs and shifting demographics. Lately, the English teachers at Champion have been stirred up by the adoption of the Common Core State Standards and worried about the requirement for more nonfiction. They have brought their concerns to the leadership team, resulting in considerable discussion about whether the English Department should stop teaching their traditional fictional literature, or whether other departments should include explicit teaching of relevant texts in their disciplines.

John finds himself taking a hard look at the substantial fiction collection in the library. He begins to gather circulation data, surveys students about their reading preferences in terms of genre and print versus electronic formats, and carefully considers the ongoing conversation among the faculty about implementation of the Common Core State Standards. He shares this information with his library advisory committee and leads them in discussions about needed library resources to support both new standards and student needs and interests.

COMMON CORE STATE STANDARDS

Developed jointly by the National Governor's Association and the Council of Chief State School Officers, the Common Core State Standards (CCSS) aim to identify desired learning outcomes for students who are college- and career-ready. These standards have been adopted, at least in part, by most states, and their impact will likely be felt in the remaining states. The standards particularly address English language arts and mathematics. Science and social studies are addressed through literacy standards developed in these content areas for grades 6–12 as part of the ELA standards. These standards feature a focus on complex texts; this focus includes a heavy emphasis on nonfiction.

School librarians have responded with attention to library collections, especially nonfiction. Many have expressed the need for short, informational texts and suggested the use of databases to fulfill this need. Others have noted the inclusion of literary nonfiction and identified this as a neglected genre in collections.

Collection-development plans and needs assessments in school systems that have adopted the CCSS should definitely attend to them. School librarians should continue to take a big-picture and long-range view in their collection-development plans. A needs assessment would certainly examine the current library collection to determine what parts of it will support these new standards. An example is the move toward using existing database subscriptions to support the need for short, informational texts.

A critical look at existing nonfiction collections for particular gaps such as narrative nonfiction is also needed. Taking into account a wide view of the needs and interests of users and of these standards and other goals of the school, the school library may also provide a strong fiction collection to balance the classroom focus on nonfiction.

Implementation of the CCSS is a good example of a circumstance in which a school librarian without a long-range collection-development plan might easily get swept up in the hype. Publishers have been quick to promote their titles as aligned with the CCSS, and numerous articles have been written about their implications for library collections. Some schools have apparently decided that the lists of text exemplars in CCSS Appendix B, however dated and lacking in diversity, should become their reading lists. Without a plan, a school librarian might be tempted to go with one of these short-term and narrow fixes to the potential long-range detriment of their users' need for a broad and diverse collection.

At Champion High School John has taken a wide-angle view inclusive of student interests and their current use of the collection. He sees a shift toward electronic books and a need to identify and develop the narrative nonfiction genre in the collection. John also recognizes that the informational databases to which Champion currently subscribes will meet the needs of both the English and other departments for more informational texts. Therefore, he asks for time at a faculty meeting to promote them and to offer to collaborate with faculty.

Using the CCSS as part of a comprehensive needs assessment will allow for the identification of existing collection resources that will serve these purposes and targeted areas for improvement. A long-range and comprehensive plan recognizes the value of the entire collection and the needs of the learning community as inclusive of numerous factors. Clearly, new national standards are a major factor to be considered. The CCSS also suggest consideration of our collections beyond books, including databases. As assessments are developed, many will be online, and another consideration for school libraries will be the inclusion of more electronic reading opportunities for students to prepare for that form of assessment. Online databases, electronic books, and other digital media may serve to fill that gap.

CONSIDERING THE NEEDS OF 21ST-CENTURY LEARNERS

Einstein Middle School is also in a state that has adopted the Common Core State Standards. The faculty members at this school find resonance with their mission statement and the CCSS's emphasis on "college and career readiness." Jean sees her principal at a school board meeting where one of the assistant superintendents is sharing results from a recent focus group of local business leaders who have expressed the need for employees who can work with others, display strong communication skills in a variety of formats, persevere to solve problems, and adapt to new technologies. The next day she slips a copy of the Standards for the 21st-Century Learner *on the principal's desk with a note about the board meeting.*

STANDARDS FOR THE 21ST-CENTURY LEARNER

School librarians also have national standards, and in our focus on our users we shouldn't neglect these standards in our needs assessments. Published in 2007, AASL's *Standards for the 21st-Century Learner* identify four learning standards and articulate skills, dispositions in action, responsibilities, and self-assessment strands that are woven throughout. These standards suggest different types of materials and tools that might be part of a school library's collection-development plan and needs assessment. How well do our collections meet the vision expressed in these learning standards? What do these standards tell us about the categories of resources and tools we should consider? Table 4 offers a look at the varieties of resources and tools implied in the learning standards.

Table 4. Types of resources and tools implied by *Standards for the 21st-Century Learner.*

Standards for the 21st-Century Learner	Does the collection include these types of resources and tools?
1. **Inquire, think critically, and gain knowledge.**	<ul><li>resources that promote critical thinking and inquiry</li><li>resources and tools to make real-world connections</li><li>resources that build background knowledge</li><li>tools for inquiry</li></ul>
2. **Draw conclusions, make informed decisions, apply knowledge to new situations, and create new knowledge.**	<ul><li>tools for organizing and analyzing information</li><li>tools for creating products</li><li>resources that provide divergent and convergent ideas</li><li>resources that provide a variety of viewpoints</li></ul>
3. **Share knowledge and participate ethically and productively as members of our democratic society.**	<ul><li>tools for collaborating and communicating</li><li>resources about local community issues</li><li>resources with diverse perspectives/ viewpoints</li><li>resources about democratic values and intellectual freedom</li></ul>
4. **Pursue personal and aesthetic growth.**	<ul><li>literature and other creative expressions in a variety of formats and genres</li><li>information related to personal interests and curiosity of students</li><li>tools for creative and artistic expression</li><li>resources that go beyond academic requirements</li><li>resources for pleasure reading</li></ul>

Clearly, reading materials are identified with libraries and continue to frame school librarians' common beliefs and standards. But a close review of these beliefs suggests that reading resources be defined as more than print text but, instead, "all formats (e.g., picture, video, print)" (AASL 2007, 2) and the identification of "multiple literacies including digital, visual, textual and technological" (AASL 2007, 3) implies that our collections should be rich sources of images, audio, and video as well as print, and that students should have access to all of these formats. A collection-development plan focused on these learning standards will include attention to a balance of formats.

Among the four AASL standards, the one that learners "pursue personal and aesthetic growth" (2007, 7) suggests that student's personal knowledge, interests, and learning are highly valued and deserve reflection in our collections. This attention to the aesthetic and individualized interests and growth of learners suggests a broader kind of collection development. On the one hand, it argues for a kind of patron-driven collection development with on-demand electronic purchases, for example. But this attention also suggests the role of the library in helping young people to develop these aesthetic and personal interests through exposure to a broad swath of topics and presentations.

Teachers at Einstein Middle School are very familiar with AASL's Standards for the 21st-Century Learner *since Jean regularly and explicitly references them during team meetings and in collaborative lesson plans. Recently, the conversations have shifted toward the kinds of learning experiences teachers might provide to promote students as producers—not just consumers. Jean begins to ponder how many of what types of tools will be needed. She leads the library advisory committee in a needs assessment that examines both content and process standards along with input from the teaching staff and their knowledge of students' abilities and interests. Jean also provides reference to the school board and business community's needs for a 21st-century workforce.*

One other predominant feature of the learning standards is the focus on access to "resources and tools" for learning within each of the four standards. Generally librarians have thought of resources as synonymous with collections. Extending our idea of collections to include "tools" suggests that our collection-development plans should not be driven just by content but also by tools needed to access content as well as the tools to create content. There is precedent in school libraries for acquiring creation-related tools, such as laminators, copy machines, and video production and editing equipment. The gap here has often been that the use of these tools was restricted to staff. Student access was limited and generally directed by adults. A needs assessment should also take into account the expectation that learners will create new knowledge. Therefore, the assessment should identify the tasks for which tools should be collected, as well as the methods by which learners could be given access to the tools.

EVALUATING THE EXISTING COLLECTION

In the process of doing a needs assessment, a librarian considers the gap between the ideal and existing conditions. Clearly, to identify the gap, the librarian must assess the existing collection. Each of the types of data discussed so far in this chapter—about the students, about the school, and about the curriculum—must be compared to the existing resources. What is available in the collection to meet the needs and interests of student X? Will student X see his or her culture, family, and interests reflected in the collection? Will the collection meet the particular learning needs and style of student X? Will the collection help student X to fulfill the school's mission, master the state or national curriculum, and acquire the skills, dispositions, responsibilities, and self-assessment strategies needed by 21st-century learners? Each of these questions might be mapped to some aspect of the collection.

Where gaps are identified, plans can be developed to fill them. Resources and tools can be identified, selected, budgeted, and purchased, and then made accessible. The process would then continue with further evaluation. Suggestions for collection mapping and other kinds of collection evaluation are discussed further in chapter 8.

LISTENING POSTS

The school librarian who is a leader demonstrates "a willingness to serve as a teacher and a learner who listens to and acts upon good ideas from peers, teachers, and students" (AASL 2009, 17). Listening is perhaps one of the most important aspects of a needs assessment. In developing a collection, the school librarian should listen to identify the needs of the learning community. Every school has particular "listening posts" where an astute leader can get a sense of the needs and pulse of a community. In the school library these listening posts include the circulation desk, the library catalog, and the library shelves.

Paying attention to what patrons ask for and search for, and listening in on conversations about reading tastes and interests provide the school librarian with leads for areas of the collection that should be developed. Do teachers walk in, look at shelves, and walk out empty-handed? What was it that they sought but didn't find? A follow-up conversation may help to identify these gaps. Engaging students in conversations about after-school interests, sports, clubs, and hobbies may also uncover needs.

Wherever teachers gather for planning, lunch, professional development, or other meetings—both informal and formal—school librarians have opportunities to listen to their needs. Bulletin boards and displays of student work provide insights into teacher styles and curriculum emphases. Parents and volunteers may serve as informants about community interests and needs. School communities change constantly. New families join the school, staff members turn over, housing patterns change, or attendance zones are redrawn. It's important to continuously assess who is part of the school's learning community.

Other more formal means of assessing needs are surveys and focus groups. A key function of a library advisory committee that consists of representatives from the various stakeholders, including staff, administrators, parents, and students, is to provide information about collection needs and input into the collection-development plan. But the librarian who is a leader and a good listener has a "with-it-ness" that allows for the identification of key questions and trends, and an ability to anticipate needs as they emerge—even before they are formally expressed. This familiarity with the learning community and the needs of individual members, along with a willingness to fulfill those needs, is a key aspect of building collections and building trust.

Each of the scenarios presented in this chapter demonstrate various listening posts including interviewing the principal; attending leadership, PTA, and school board meetings; taking an active part in leading a library advisory committee; and collaborating with teams of teachers. Sarah, John, and Jean are all listening carefully for the needs and interests of their students as well as curriculum standards.

REFLECTIVE QUESTIONS

▶ What types of listening posts can I identify in my library, school, and community?

▶ What would a needs assessment look like through the lens of one student?

▶ What types of tools would I add to the collection to meet the *Standards for the 21st-Century Learner*?

▶ How can I identify and tag specialized genres such as "narrative non-fiction" in the library catalog?

▶ Do I consider the content in databases as part of our collection-development plan? What are the issues relating to learners' access to this resource?

▶ School communities change over time and traces of previous community needs persist in library collections. What evidence do I see in the collection of past demographics or other characteristics?

Chapter 4

What Should We Collect?
And How Do We Select?

WHAT TO COLLECT

What should we collect? It's really a lovely question evocative of childhood collections of rocks, seashells, and bird feathers, or address books filled with family members, high school friends, and local services like hairdressers or doctors. Collecting is a very human activity, and librarians are respected and consulted for their skill at collecting books and other resources that are valuable and useful to a community. Librarians have refined the art to include selection, classification, and arrangement of those resources to promote access to high-quality and broad perspectives. In school libraries, rock collections and databases of local and national contacts also have a place beside print and digital resources. In this chapter we look in more detail at the kinds of questions Sarah must consider as she prepares to open a new collection, the types of materials to include in the library collection and how to select them.

As Sarah begins working on the selection of materials for the new school, she must decide how to dis-

tribute the funding she receives to purchase print and non-print materials. She finds that the library budget has been allocated to fund a very traditional school library with books, magazines, and reference materials in print and electronic formats. Access to some databases and a video streaming service will be provided by the school system. Sarah starts to make a list of the other types of materials the school community will need, including audiobooks, DVDs, and professional books and materials for teachers. Some of the teachers have expressed an interest in apps to use with students. Several of these formats will also require equipment to access. Sarah is determined that the audiovisual resources will not remain in a closet but will be accessible to students as well as staff.

In conversations with her principal, Sarah learns that he is determined that other instructional materials such as math and science manipulatives will also circulate through the library. Sarah begins to look at the science and social studies curricula to determine what types of realia might be needed, such as models of the solar system or parts of a plant. She believes that physical maps and globes will be important for young learners in addition to the digital forms of these resources.

Teachers talk about opening the school as a collaborative team, planning and sharing lesson ideas with one another. Sarah suggests they curate their lesson plans and create an electronic dropbox with folders for grade levels and subject areas. Creating a password-protected space will also allow students' work samples to be uploaded.

The new school has created a lot of interest in the community; Sarah begins to build a spreadsheet with community organizations and individuals who have expressed an interest in the school. Sarah takes her list of instructional materials to her principal and the leadership team along with the budget she has been allocated. Teachers are excited about the possibilities and begin to identify funding sources beyond the library allocation. Table 5 shows the types of materials and potential funding sources.

By carefully attending to the needs and interests expressed by her principal and teachers, Sarah has widened the definition of the school's library collection. She has also successfully widened the funding possibilities for the collection, as well as garnering some attention to time and staffing needs to fulfill the shared vision. Perhaps the most important thing she has accomplished is a foundation of collaboration. She has demonstrated her attention to the curriculum and the teaching preferences of the teachers; they, in turn, recognize her value as a collaborative partner. Sarah has provided her princi-

Table 5. Types of materials and potential funding sources.

Types of Materials	Potential Funding
books, magazines, reference materials in print and non-print	library allocation
databases and video streaming	school system
audiobooks, DVDs, apps	library allocation/general instructional funds
equipment for students to use audiobooks, DVDs, apps (classrooms will be equipped)	PTA or community grant funds
math and science manipulatives and models; maps and globes	general instructional funds
professional books and other materials	professional-development funds
shared lesson plans and a dropbox in which to make them accessible	Time will be allocated for collaborative planning and sharing of lessons; dropbox will be supported by school system.
database of community contacts	Principal agrees to provide hours for office assistant to facilitate creation of this important resource.

pal and leadership team with projected costs and resources needed to support the learning needs of the school community. Next, she will expand the plan by identifying and selecting specific items for the collection in time to acquire the resources by opening day.

HOW TO SELECT

Numerous established and authoritative selection aids exist for print materials; several are listed in Appendix C. Consider the source of review; some may have a sales focus or be aimed at a non-library audience such as parents. Personal examination of resources is helpful when possible and may be the only way to decide about realia or equipment. School librarians can also draw on the expertise and advice of teachers or visit vendors at conferences. Reviews of DVDs, audiobooks, and electronic databases and tools including apps are not as ubiquitous as those for book, but these reviews also exist (see Appendix C).

A challenge for the school librarian will be in applying selection criteria to ever-changing new formats. In her book *The Collection Program in Schools* Kay Bishop included an excellent chapter on selection criteria applied to various formats (2013, 71–103), and her chapter "General Selection Criteria" (61–69) is an excellent overview of selection criteria. Regardless of format, general selection criteria regarding the authority, the content, the media, the user, and the collection will always apply. These criteria cannot be considered in isolation but rather intersect and interact with each other in meaningful ways. For example, questions about authority relate to the authorship and producers of the item and their credentials and experience with the subject matter or content and with the format. A poorly edited book, or a book with a weak binding, might not be a good selection despite the author's expertise with the subject matter. The issue of a producer's experience and expertise working with a format is important with newly emerging formats. A producer may rush a product with new technology to market before the bugs have been worked out. Table 6 shows a crosswalk of selection criteria and how they intersect with each other.

COST

Cost is also a consideration in selection and acquisition, but cost is not a straightforward issue. Most items come with additional costs beyond initial purchase price. Books need processing that includes applying barcodes and protective covers, and creating cataloging records. Paperbacks may require extra protection through a publisher's binding or other reinforcement. Many items need packaging to keep the parts together and/or to protect the item. Hanging bags, cases, or other kinds of packaging may be needed. An item may need special shelving or storage such as charging carts for tablets or e-readers. Many media require additional equipment for e-reading, listening, or viewing.

Need for special equipment and concern about costs have been reasons used in the past to limit access to an item. However, as costs come down for tablets and e-readers (and more students—in some communities—have access to such equipment outside of school), the price of tools needed to access e-resources should be less of a barrier. If we think of the cost of an item as calculated on a per-use basis, then restricting access only raises the cost per use.

Table 6. Crosswalk of selection criteria.

	authority	content	presentation	user	collection value
authority	The creators (author, publisher, producer) of the item have demonstrated authority.	Evidence that the author, publisher, producer has knowledge or expertise related to the content.	The illustrator, designer, author, producer, publisher has experience with this format.	The creators have experience or other knowledge about the intended audience.	Item fills a need for authoritative perspective in the collection.
content		Content is high-quality, current, accurate and has clear scope.	Arrangement or sequence or presentation is appropriate to content. Adds value or meaning to content.	Content is developmentally, intellectually, emotionally appropriate for the intended user.	Item fills a content or perspective on content needed in the collection.
presentation			Medium is used effectively.	Accessible for the user.	Item fills an access or format need in the collection.
user				Item is appealing and meets needs and interests of particular users.	Item fills a user need in the collection.
collection value					Item contributes something original to the collection or meets demand for multiple users.

SELECTION FOR SPECIFIC LEARNERS

A primary question related to selection is the match between the item and the user. No matter how homogeneous a school appears, wide differences in developmental, intellectual, and emotional readiness for content or format will exist. Content issues might include the student's background knowledge or experiences with the subject. Format issues could relate to reading level, need for audio enhancement, or small motor skills required by a piece of technology. Every school year brings new students with new interests.

Sarah remembers the student who arrived at her school and wanted informational books on fishing, and the year a teacher arrived from New Zealand and his students wanted books with photographs of his home country. Sarah has identified another user need in her consideration of allowing students to access various media formats. She recognizes that the population of the new school is unlikely to possess e-readers, tablets, or audio devices needed to access many of the formats. Her collection plan must also include hardware and containers for the various formats.

Just as librarians have always recognized that books get wear and tear, and, therefore, reinforce paperbacks or put Mylar jackets on hardcover books, today's librarians will need to consider cases that will protect devices during transport in bookbags and other typical hazards.

As Sarah gets ready to prepare orders for her new school, she knows she will want to have a variety of formats to appeal to the students she expects to serve and to support her teachers in the curriculum she knows they will be teaching. At first she thinks about the print collection. She expects to have a collection that includes picture books, easy-to-read books for emerging readers, transitional books for those just getting ready for chapter books, and chapter books. But she also decides that a collection of board books might be important for the preschool students and the families she hopes to attract to the library. Her primary teachers are accustomed to using "big books" in the classroom as visual aids for reading instruction, but she knows the new classrooms will have interactive whiteboards and wonders about digital books that might be projected on those boards. Will the teachers still need as many big books? She's also curious about adding more graphic novels to the collection.

As she considers her magazine, nonfiction, and reference collections, she wonders if more digital books and databases will replace some of those and how much? Sarah is also wondering about electronic books and what balance she should consider in terms of their acquisition—particularly as she expects her students will not have devices to read them. Her preschool teachers are excited about some of the book apps they have seen demonstrated in interactive story times with young children. The more she thinks about alternative digital formats for books, the more she wonders about them. Would those transitional readers benefit from an e-book that includes pronunciation and a dictionary? Will formats like the picture book and the popular graphic novels transfer to electronic formats? And what about access for her students? Sarah decides to start by offering access in the library to e-books and book apps through a browsing basket of tablets loaded with selected apps and interactive e-books. She also decides to seek funding to purchase a touch table that will allow small-group access to these books and apps in a manner that is developmentally appropriate.

Decisions like Sarah's about school library collections are tightly interwoven with the instructional focus of the school, and on the learners in the school and their communities. Selection decisions are driven not just by the qualities of the selected items, but by their match with the mission, curriculum, and students in the school. These are local decisions driven by local needs and interests. No one is in a better position to make these decisions than a professionally trained school librarian. School librarians have listening posts not only throughout the school community, but in the worlds of publishing, producing, and technology. Today's technologies invite fulfillment through patron profiles or patron-driven choices.

However, school librarians have a larger vision. They see the big picture of the school's curriculum, the school's community, and the availability of resources. Their perspective widens that of teachers who may see their grade level only or textbook-driven selections. School librarians widen the developing tastes and interests of students to include other perspectives and genres. A school librarian understands the true costs associated with providing access to various formats as well as the costs of denying access to the best resource to meet a particular need for information.

WEB RESOURCES

Collection development in the twenty-first century is also about selecting, acquiring, and providing access to websites. An important partner to collection development is the cataloging, classification, and shelving of materials to provide access to users at their point of need. Therefore, curating websites and other tools available via the Internet begins to look as much like good cataloging as good selection. Selection narrows the universe of available materials to those deemed most appropriate for the library's community.

Today's challenge is not information scarcity but information overload. In such a context, selection of the best from the universe of what's available provides an invaluable service for a library's community. The same selection criteria that librarians have applied for generations continue to be relevant.

When the selection process is applied to collections of websites, this provision of targeted access provides a type of metadata or cataloging that adds value to the selection. As Sarah begins to create folders of videos on the video-streaming site that she recognizes as targeted to specific grade-level curricula, she is performing both selection through her judgment about the match with content and users, and a classification that provides better access for her teachers and students.

Many of today's students and even teachers have the perception that Google is the ultimate search tool for their purposes. As school librarians begin to develop targeted collections of websites, they provide a valuable service and model for students.

ACCESS TO E-RESOURCES

Ideally, the school's online catalog will become a go-to resource for student informational and recreational interests and needs. Therefore, school librarians should begin to explore cataloging options that allow the seamless integration of access to e-books, databases, and websites. As student interests become more specialized, learners will need access to experts in their field as resources and potential audiences for their projects. A database like Sarah's spreadsheet of interested community partners becomes a selective and organized tool for schools.

SUPPORT FOR 21ST-CENTURY STUDENTS

Today's library collections serve to mediate the needs and interests of today's students with the kinds of information resources available today. Effective collections offer multiple resources in multiple formats to meet today's diverse students. Formats are selected to address student needs as the best format to deliver the content to a particular student. Appropriateness of format is dependent on both the content and the individual needs of students. A model of the parts of a plant may be the best way for many primary children to experience this concept that is both visual and tactile. For many young children the printed and bound book may be the best format to experience a picture book because the pictures, page turns, and book design are key to the experience. However, for other children a more accessible format may be an audio version of the text or an electronic version that includes some animation, read-aloud functionality, and assistance with text by means of definitions displayed as words are clicked.

The professionally trained school librarian has the perspective to fully consider how to match available formats with content and with students. The best selection decisions look at students as individuals with individual needs and preferences, and are intended to build a collection to meet the full diversity of a school. A variety of formats must be considered to meet the diverse needs and interests of a school community. Table 7 lists some of the types of materials Sarah and other school librarians should consider for their collections.

Table 7. Types of non-book materials to consider for school library collections.

Types of Materials School Librarians Might Collect
e-reading devices
databases
URLs of websites
experts' e-mail addresses and Skype i.d.'s
local experts' phone numbers and addresses, areas of interest
realia
models
manipulatives
productivity and creation tools, especially digital and specialized equipment
measurement devices
software
student-created work
teachers' lesson plans
collaborative units
audio resources
video resources
equipment to access/produce (microphones, speakers, projectors, screens)
maps
art prints
portable greenhouse
aquaria/terraria
simple machines
simple tools (hammers, screwdrivers, etc.)
electrical wires, batteries, etc.

REFLECTIVE QUESTIONS

▶ Does our collection provide the widest possible access to information in a variety of formats?

▶ Are some areas of the collection are restricted to particular patrons? Is the basis for their restriction valid?

▶ If a new format were to come on board tomorrow, would we be able to apply the same selection criteria in use now?

▶ What are the hidden costs associated with "free" materials? (packaging, equipment, staff time, replacements)

▶ Might resources in some area of our collection-development plan be funded through other allocations?

▶ What role does our library advisory committee, school leadership committees, or parent-teacher organization play in the collection-development plan?

Chapter 5

What Is a Book?

WEALTH OF OPTIONS

Today's digital formats have begun to challenge traditional understanding of what a book is. The paper book is a versatile, portable, and convenient format. It has endured even as new electronic formats/media have come into being; these e-formats are also "books."

But even when focusing only on physical books, a variety of formats must be considered: picture books, easy-to-read books, transitional books, graphic novels, and chapter books. Books come in different shapes and sizes that have presented shelving issues: "big books" intended as visual aids during storytelling and for reading instruction, oversized coffee table books, reference books, and tiny books like the Beatrix Potter series. Books come in different bindings: library, trade, paper, board, and, sometimes, spiral. Some books, such as paperbacks and pop-up or lift-the-flap books, fall apart with repeated use. Each of these formats must be considered for collections, and they present a variety of challenges ranging from how to shelve to how to circulate. A summary of some book formats and their limitations for library collections is presented in table 8.

Library collections have always had a "paper problem." In addition to the book formats, libraries have collected magazines and newspapers, pamphlets and other ephemera, maps, and art prints. Many of these formats were not as enduring as a book. Some, like the newspaper, may not have been retained long. Magazines are usually not retained for more than a few months (and only for recreational reading) now that online databases provide access that includes indexing to past issues. Many school libraries have responded to this change by allowing magazines to circulate. Art prints and maps have been replaced with digital slides, and interactive and online maps, but elementary teachers still value the tactile presence of prints and maps when introducing them to young children.

Books have long had a history of sliding into other formats. We can all name popular books that became full-length movies. But picture books have long been adapted to filmstrip, sound filmstrip, sixteen-millimeter film, VHS and DVD video formats, and now streaming videos online. Books on tape, or audiobooks, have also been a school library staple, but were often restricted to classroom or in-library use. Along with electronic books, the ability to easily download an audiobook and even to synch the audiobook with the e-book have made this format increasingly popular and mainstream. School librarians today continue to consider these audio formats for their collections and to provide access to students as well as teachers.

A key difference today is the convergence of audiobooks and e-books into digital forms that can potentially be accessed from a single, personal device. Increasingly, the cell phone students in middle school and high school carry in their pockets is one of the devices that allows this access to all kinds of media, including electronic books. However, students in Sarah's elementary school are less likely to bring these sophisticated devices to school. Younger children don't have the small motor skills to easily use them, and their parents are reluctant to send children out of the house with these expensive devices—or cannot afford the devices. Older students may have a variety of devices with a variety of data plans that make online access or downloads more prohibitive because of expense.

TRANSITION STRATEGIES

At Champion High School John faces questions about how to begin introducing electronic books to the collection. Increasingly, Champion students bring to school devices that support e-books. Learners' first choice for research is to search the Web through their devices. John is uncertain where to begin with e-book acquisition. He decides to look at the most-circulated print items and considers extra copies in digital formats that will allow multiple readers simultaneous access to the book. John has a good knowledge of the tastes of his students and trends in young adult literature. He is usually able to anticipate which new titles will be in high demand. As he puts together a new book order, he considers purchasing many of these fiction titles in electronic formats to meet demands.

Similar demands have been placed on the library program by departmental needs for class sets of books such as Steinbeck's Of Mice and Men. *John suggests at departmental meetings that departments consider purchasing several of these required reads in electronic formats with licenses for unlimited multiple users. The departments are excited by this prospect because in the past they have chosen books for a whole-school read, and now they may consider the possibility that everyone in this large school could access the selection as an e-book.*

As John looks at circulation data for the most popular books, he sees another potential area for e-books: the least circulated, more-specialized nonfiction that the library acquires to support individual senior research projects. Much of this purchasing of specialized nonfiction has already been replaced with access to extensive databases, but John begins to wonder whether purchasing or leasing e-books would be more cost- and space-effective for titles that may be needed by only one or two students and for limited time periods.

Even at schools like Champion where it seems like every student in the school owns at least a smartphone, some students do not have access to devices or data plans that enable e-book access. School librarians need to advocate for these students even if they represent a small minority in a school. Plus, teenagers are notorious for losing, forgetting, or not charging their devices. Even the most privileged and technologically equipped students will sometimes need to use school-provided devices. Teachers and administrators realized this reality as soon as BYOD was implemented at Champion.

As school libraries move their collections to electronic books and classrooms use e-books for in-class reading assignments and homework, schools

Table 8. Book formats and considerations for library collections.

Book Packages	Definition	Benefits	Issues
library hardcover	Pages are bound between boards. This is a publisher designation that generally means binding is reinforced for library use.	Bindings may be more durable than other hardcovers. Some vendors offer a discount on this reinforced binding for libraries.	Book jackets need protection and must be secured to books. This format may be more expensive to produce and reinforcement quality varies.
trade hardcover	Pages are bound between boards.	Binding is more durable than paperback.	Book jackets need protection and must be secured to books. Binding quality varies widely.
trade paperback	Book has paperback cover but larger trim size than mass-market paperbacks.	Lower cost. Lighter weight and more compact than hardcover for readers.	Binding and cover are not durable and, for library use, must be reinforced (or purchased with vendor-applied durable cover.
mass-market paperback	Mass-market paperbacks have "pocket" trim size.		
pre-bound paperback (e.g., Perma-Bound)	The cover is removed from a paperback book and strengthened with vinyl; book is rebound.	Binding is very durable (often guaranteed) and cost is lower than hardcover.	Because pages' paper quality is not as high as in hardcover books, pre-bound paperbacks wear out more quickly.
reinforced publisher binding (e.g., Bound to Stay Bound)	The cover is removed from a hardcover book. New, long-lasting cover and binding are applied.	Binding is very durable.	The new cover might be less attractive than the original cover design.
paperback with protective covering	Without removing the cover, vendors apply vinyl covering to paperback books.	Many of the same benefits as paperback books with somewhat better durability.	The binding and pages are still subject to wear and tear.

spiral or comb binding	Books are bound with plastic-coated wire or with plastic combs (e.g., cookbooks, how-to books).	Spiral binding is easy to lay flat, (e.g. to follow instructions or a recipe).	The pages fall out easily and are extremely difficult to reinsert.
board book	The cover and pages are cardboard, making pages durable for young readers.	Pages are easier for very young readers to turn without tearing.	The bindings wear out.
stapled (saddle-stitched)	Big books, magazines, and some reading series books are stapled in the fold.	Each of these formats have advantages, or fill a need for instructional materials, that may outweigh the weakness of the binding.	Staples wear out or tear out; though re-stapling is possible, usually special equipment is required.
audiobooks	Text of book is read aloud and recorded for distribution on cassettes, CDs, or digitally.	The audio may be more accessible for individuals or groups or in particular contexts (e.g. while mobile).	A device is required for playback and quality of narrator varies. Tests are sometimes abridged.
e-books	The content of a book has been digitized or was created for digital delivery.	E-book titles are often available on demand; multiple titles can be loaded and carried on a single device. Some support may be provided to readers (e.g. word look-up or read-aloud).	A device is required to view. Utility varies widely from page capture that requires zooming and panning on some devices to text that can be reflowed and adapted (font choice and size).
enhanced e-books	E-books that contain more than the text of the original can include links to other media, maps, and other textual information.	The reading experience may be enhanced through multimedia or links to supplementary material.	A device is required and enhancement increases prices.

(cont.)

Table 8. Book formats and considerations for library collections *(cont.)*.

Book Packages	Definition	Benefits	Issues
book apps	A book's content has been enhanced with interactive features that allow the user to "play."	The reading experience may be enhanced through interactive features.	A device is required. Extra features may be distracting. The content of the original book may be significantly changed.

must purchase devices and wrestle with the questions about how to circulate these items. As prices come down on devices, the per-use and per-title costs lower as well. In fact, schools license access to e-books that is independent of the device; if something happens to the device, the school still has access to the e-book. Over time, replacing lost or damaged devices may cost less than the expense of replacing and processing hardcover books.

NO ONE "RIGHT" FORMAT

The traditional print format of the book will continue to serve many of our students by providing tactile access to the book for new and emerging readers as well as a portable format that does not require batteries or electricity and enables easy access for everyone everywhere. The physical book may continue to be the preferred format for pleasure reading, providing relief from the work on screens that increasingly predominates our workplaces and classrooms.

Electronic books have issues related to user access. On the one hand, they can offer more access to more users simultaneously. On the other hand, reliance on e-books and other e-resources may limit access for users who have difficulty reading text in this format. Developmental and other learning differences may make electronic text difficult for very young readers or for students with visual or perceptual impairments. Some students may also prefer the printed texts. The choice to purchase a title only as an e-book may be a barrier that must be addressed for some users. The addition of a read-aloud feature may help to mediate this barrier. This issue has been raised relative to the rights of patrons with disabilities (Leverkus and Acedo 2013, 63–64).

The needs of students in each of these scenarios suggest a need for access to resources in multiple formats, including print, audiobooks, and various e-books formats. Popular fiction continues to be purchased in all formats. Needs for specialized content may dictate purchase of one format or the other. The developmental or various learning differences among students, as well as personal preferences for reading in one format or another, will continue to suggest the need for a library to offer multiple formats. Some formats, such as picture books and graphic novels, may be best presented in bound formats.

Yet the growing popularity and ease of e-books, including their adoption by teachers as textbooks, signals the need for increasing attention to this format and the issues they raise. Classroom use of books for shared reading, whether the shared reading of a single text or through multiple copies of the same book, could easily move into more digital formats projected onto a screen or delivered through e-readers. As these formats become more ubiquitous in classrooms, they widen the divide between students who have and do not have access to these instructional materials beyond the classroom because they lack the device or network access to do so. For years school libraries promulgated this divide by restricting access to formats such as audiobooks or videos to teacher checkout.

Schools face an important dilemma. The families of students may not all have robust access to the technologies needed to access electronic books, and so it would be possible to argue that learners would best be served by a print collection. Yet limited access to digital formats will continue to exacerbate the divide those students encounter as they move through their school years and into the workforce. School librarians will have to wrestle with these questions as they seek to distribute resources among print and digital formats for the library and classroom. The school librarian is in a position to lead these important discussions.

FINDING THE BALANCE

Finding the appropriate balance in formats has always been a challenge for school librarians. For example, librarians in elementary schools had to decide how many picture books, how many easy-reading titles, how many fiction versus nonfiction titles to buy. In high schools, budgets had to cover reference books to support research, narrative fiction and nonfiction—plus science, history, and news magazines—to support curriculum, and materials for pleasure reading on topics that were sometimes of only passing interest to students. These were not easy choices, but we made the best decisions based on what we knew about the curriculum, our students' needs and interests, our teachers, and the school community.

These decisions about e-book and print book acquisitions are really no different. A balanced collection has always been a moving target and always required consideration of the question of access. If every book we had about cars and trucks was on a fifth-grade reading level with few pictures, we were not providing access to the first-grade student wild about the topic. The same could be said today about the student who doesn't have access to a device for using e-resources; the difference is that the first-grader's developmental and reading ability were in many ways beyond our control while access to devices can be within our control.

REFLECTIVE QUESTIONS

▶ What formats do my students need to accommodate various developmental or learning styles?

▶ What formats are available for the content needed to support the curriculum, student inquiry, and reading interests?

▶ What formats do students prefer?

▶ Does some content work better in one format than in another?

▶ On what bases will resources—including e-resources—be weeded?

▶ What devices or accessories are needed by individuals to access e-resources? By whole classes reading simultaneously in classrooms?

▶ Do some formats restrict access for some patrons?

Chapter 6

Supporting Creation, Dissemination, and Community

NEW SLANT ON OLD RESPONSIBILITY

Libraries have always been creation spaces. Reading is an active and creative process. When libraries consisted almost exclusively of printed texts, they offered the quiet spaces needed for the solitary work of readers engaging with written texts to actively create meaning from those texts. As other media were added to libraries, equipment, and spaces were added for the consumption of those items. Patrons were handed headphones or directed to separate rooms to engage with audio and preserve the quiet space for readers.

The mission of the school library to "ensure that students and staff are effective users of ideas and information" clearly supports the continuing work of patrons to create meaning as consumers of ideas and information. However, in today's media-rich information environment, effective users not only consume information and ideas, they effectively produce their own knowledge creations. Today's school library will provide spaces for all of these kinds of creative work, ranging from quiet, solitary reading to collaborative group work, to the active creation of individual and group products. Today's collections must also support this range of creative endeavors with both content and tools but also through the provisions of the resources needed to connect students with the school and wider communities through effective dissemination of learners' creations.

WHY WE NEED TO COLLECT TOOLS

AASL's *Standards for the 21st-Century Learner* support helping students develop real-world connections and create new knowledge. These standards provide guidance for the types of resources and tools that today's students will need for learning. School librarians often use standards in the content areas of mathematics, language arts, science, or social studies, for example, to guide selection of resources in a variety of formats to deliver and support those curriculum areas. But what about the types of resources and tools for which AASL's standards imply a need? What tools do students need to "inquire, think critically, and gain knowledge" (AASL 2007, 3)? Are apps or other tools available that will allow them to "develop and refine a range of questions to frame the search for new understanding" (1.1.3)? What types of communication tools do they need to "contribute to the exchange of ideas within the learning community" (1.3.4), and what types of technology would best assist them to "seek appropriate help when it is needed" (1.4.4)? Do we have sufficient variety of resources to allow them to "demonstrate creativity by using multiple resources and formats" (1.2.3)?

What would a collection look like if we were truly guided by these standards? Clearly it would include sufficient reading materials, with reading interpreted broadly as "text in all formats (e.g., picture, video, print) and all contexts" (AASL 2007, 2). The word "tools" is also sprinkled throughout the common beliefs and the learning standards. Table 9 shows the particular standards that mention technology and other information tools for accessing, pursuing, analyzing, organizing, displaying, understanding, gathering and sharing information from across each of the four standards.

Among the common beliefs expressed is "school libraries are essential to the development of learning skills," with the explication "school libraries provide equitable physical and intellectual access to resources and tools required

Table 9. References to tools in the skills in *Standards for the 21st-Century Learner.*

	Skills
1.1.8	Demonstrate mastery of technology tools for accessing information and pursing inquiry.
2.1.4	Use technology and other information tools to analyze and organize information.
3.1.4	Use technology and other information tools to organize and display knowledge and understanding in ways that others can view, use, and access.
4.1.7	Use social networks and information tools to gather and share information.

for learning in a warm, stimulating, and safe environment" (AASL 2007, 3). Our standards suggest that we will identify, select, and collect tools as well as information resources.

At Einstein Middle School, Jean's collaborative work with teachers has led her to realize that the library collection should include tools for students to use as they gather and share information. Jean's principal is convinced that the school system mission to educate students to be productive citizens and members of the workforce aligns well with the Standards for the 21st-Century Learner; *he supports Jean in numerous conversations with teachers and parents about the role of the school library in developing students who are producers not just consumers of information. Stakeholders see the school library as a creation space where students can learn to use media in their own productions.*

PROVIDING ACCESS TO TOOLS

School libraries have often provided teachers with access to tools, such as copy machines, die-cut machines, laminators, and book binders, all of which facilitated teacher-created materials for bulletin boards and instruction. As such, these tools joined the other types of resources that in the past were restricted to teachers. A few exceptions were made; for example, a student club might have had access to video equipment for recorded or live student broadcasts. Schools may have acquired specialized photography equipment or a darkroom, or specialized video and sound editing equipment. These items were considered equipment rather than part of the library's circulating collection. They may have found their way to student work or clubs, but their use was directed by teachers. Students rarely had unfettered access to these tools for their own creations.

In today's complex information environment, we can't afford to overlook these productivity tools in our plans for student learning. We must consider providing access beyond just faculty or student clubs.

COLLECTING AND SELECTING TOOLS

With the proliferation of audio and video tools designed to run on hand-held devices, including the ubiquitous smartphone, many students are already using these devices as tools to capture and post images, audio, and videos. Schools could build upon these skills by integrating these tools and products into classrooms and school libraries by teaching students to effectively create, document, and share their learning. The school library can serve to offer more-specialized apps or tools to facilitate these productions and make them core to the instructional focus of the school. School libraries might collect equipment and software for capturing and editing audio and video.

Selection of tools for creating products that do not rely solely on the written word is challenging. At the state conference for school librarians, Jean visits vendors to explore video- and audio-editing equipment and software for the school. She is able to try out some of the equipment or see it demonstrated at the exhibits. Among other tools, she decides to acquire external microphones. When learners try out the new mics, they are pleased with the improved the sound quality in video productions, of course. As a bonus, experimenting with the mics spurs interest in podcasting.

Many of these new tools and applications also make demands on technology infrastructure. Jean recognizes the need for more outlets and charging stations in the school library. File handling and storage of large audio and video files also becomes an issue. She approaches the district IT team for advice on how to meet these needs. Some of the recommendations would be too costly to implement now. However, she is pleasantly surprised to learn that her students' productions can be stored on a district server networked to a workstation in her library.

Many productivity and creation tools can be found on the Web or as apps for hand-held devices. Jean consults annual lists such as AASL's lists of Best Websites for Teaching and Learning, and Best Apps for Teaching and Learning to identify potential resources to use with school-owned devices. She also makes teachers, students, and parents aware of e-resources that are free or low cost.

Access is a huge concern at Einstein Middle School. Jean and the faculty collaborate to provide access for students to work on classroom projects. Faculty members have realized the need for extended access to devices and equipment for all students—but particularly for those who might not have access at home. The library is open before and after school, and plans are made to staff the library two evenings a week year-round, including breaks and summers. Community and peer volunteers are solicited to provide mentoring and other assistance with media creations.

The same kinds of selection criteria discussed in chapter 4 should be applied to equipment and other kinds of tools. For example, it's important to consider the experience the manufacturer has with this sort of technology and the type of user support provided. Clearly, the scope of the functions a tool performs and how well a tool performs are necessary considerations. Additionally, school librarians must consider what other kinds of resources are needed (devices, networks, power) to effectively use the tool. The initial cost is only one consideration because additional costs may be associated with the maintenance and continued use of the tool. Costs should be weighed against the value the tool adds to the collection, both in terms of how it will be used and whether it duplicates a function performed by another tool already available through the library.

TYPES OF REAL-WORLD TOOLS

As school librarians ponder what kinds of tools to collect, we might think about the real-world connections we want to make for students. What are the kinds of tools needed in today's work, recreation, and home spaces? Tools might include microscopes, weather instruments, or probeware needed to provide students with science experiences. Or tools might be cameras, microphones, and editing software for a broadcast or the creation of augmented reality.

School librarians might also have an eye toward more cutting-edge and expensive kinds of equipment that other types of libraries are looking at such as 3-D printers or machines that print and bind books on demand. But school libraries could also provide students with materials and space for low-tech sharing: paper, glue sticks, staplers, and scissors, and access to a copy machine or laminator. School library programs can catch the do-it-yourself trend with a knitting or carpentry club, or provide space and resources for a robotics club. (Community members may be willing to share their expertise with members of the clubs.) Traditional book and periodical collections can also support these initiatives if the librarian selects related books and magazines or how-to videos.

COLLECTION AND DISSEMINATION OF STUDENT CREATIONS

As school librarians collect the tools that students will need to become effective producers of knowledge, librarians must also consider how to assist students in publishing or disseminating their creations. For example, students collecting weather data might share it with a local news outlet. The school librarian's collection of community resources can connect students to the expertise of community members but can also serve to connect the expertise of students to the community.

At Einstein Middle School, Jean recognizes the need to collect and to disseminate student projects. When the journalism club decides to go digital and create an online e-zine of student writing, their work has the potential to reach a much larger audience than previous publications of the club. While Einstein Middle School has drawn on community expertise for many projects, students are also beginning to contribute their own expertise to the community. This sharing was underscored by the eighth-grade project for which students interviewed residents from the area who were Holocaust survivors or family members of survivors. Jean worked with teachers and students to collect the video and audio interviews, photographs of artifacts, and the student research about the history and geography related to the stories and items. Learners' work was recognized and featured by a local history museum.

NEW OPPORTUNITIES

The shifts occurring in education and libraries today offer unique opportunities for school librarians and their programs. We have a mission and standards that direct us to equip students to contribute to the broader learning community beyond the school. As parts of our collections shift to digital formats, we may find ourselves with empty shelves and open spaces. These provide opportunities for us to shift our focus from the consumption of knowledge to the active creation of new knowledge. A similar shift must occur in our collections to offer tools and access to tools for media creations and their dissemination. We are building collections, but we are also building connections for our students and the learning community.

REFLECTIVE QUESTIONS

▶ What types of tools could my library collect?

▶ What types of tools are housed in my library but limited to use by teachers?

▶ What materials and tools are needed to implement the *Standards for the 21st-Century Learner*?

▶ What is the role of the school library in the collection and dissemination of student-created work?

Chapter 7

E-Book Acquisitions and Devices

NOTE: Given the technical content of this chapter, definitions of some terms, which are bolded when introduced, are provided in a glossary at the end of the chapter.

CHALLENGE AND OPPORTUNITY

Perhaps no shift in library collections has been as unsettling as the shift toward e-books and other electronic forms of information. In school libraries, this shift offers both challenges and opportunities as electronic formats both increase access and raise issues related to equity of access for all students. Electronic formats do not get used up in the same way that a physical book or item does. More than one person can access an electronic book at the same time. An electronic book may circulate hundreds or thousands of times without wear and tear while a physical book would require rebinding, multiple copies and replacements. These factors have strong appeal for school library collections because classrooms, departments, or grade levels frequently require students to simultaneously study the same content and frequently the same book, for example when a grade level is studying Huckleberry Finn. These assignments may endure for years putting heavy demand on collections. Various licensing and purchase plans for electronic books, including the availability of free e-books, open opportunities for school libraries to improve access. The challenges will be navigating the various acquisition and licensing plans. One further challenge for school libraries will be the types and numbers of devices needed to access these electronic materials. This chapter will discuss strategies to address these two challenges for school libraries committed to providing equitable access for all students: acquisitions of e-books and the need for e-reading devices. As more content shifts to digital formats, issues of acquisitions and patron access will continue to impact collection development for school libraries.

ACQUISITIONS OF E-BOOKS

Sarah prepares to order resources for the new school library. While print books in all of their variety will be purchased and owned by the school, the purchasing plans for e-books and access to other e-resources look very different; in fact, she is faced with a dizzying array of purchasing models from outright ownership of e-books to **short-term leases** *and long-term* **licenses.** *Several purchasing models will have budget implications beyond the opening of the school.*

Sarah's school district has purchased a license to a basic set of e-books. The licensing for these e-books is very generous allowing **unlimited users,** *but the selection of books is very small. Sarah's school can purchase its own e-books to add to this selection. The costs of these added books vary, depending on the license selected for each. An advantage Sarah recognizes for e-books is the potential for multiple people to read the same book at the same time, but she discovers a range of licensing possibilities from* **unlimited, to multiple user, to single use.**

Additionally, Sarah discovers some appealing nonfiction choices that can be streamed to desktop or mobile devices. These electronic resources include multimedia and will be updated regularly with new content (Bacon 2013b). Licensing for this content looks like the **subscription** *costs of electronic databases. Sarah realizes that some of her opening-year purchases will pay only for a year's access to many of these electronic resources. The choices she makes now may have long-term implications for her school and the school library's budget. Sarah reads the fine print in all the plans she is seriously considering.*

20TH-CENTURY PLANS

A collection-development plan has always been about more than a single year. Periodical and other subscriptions had to be renewed. Lost or damaged materials had to be replaced. Some materials had to be weeded from the collection, and plans included the purchase of new, relevant, and current materials. Schools owned the materials they had purchased. Because the shelves were full of books from better-funded years, in tough economic times the library program could manage to survive a year with a slim budget that did little more than maintain the periodical subscriptions.

In the past, libraries were defined by what they owned. Collections were evaluated based on the number of volumes and, perhaps, the age of the volumes. Books and other materials had a physical presence with stamps of ownership on each. Items weeded from the collection were the library's to discard, give away, or sell as used copies.

21ST-CENTURY PLANS AND E-RESOURCES

The current electronic landscape opens new questions about ownership and access. Ideally, a collection-development plan contains objectives the librarian can keep in mind when faced with an array of acquisition models. Most look more like a license to lease titles rather than outright ownership. Sue Polanka has cited Kevin Kelly from *Wired* magazine as stating the future of publishing looks more like access than ownership (Polanka 2013, 65), and she discussed various subscription and collection models emerging in the consumer market and likely to impact the library landscape.

Many of the decisions that Sarah faces were described by Polanka in 2011; though Polanka suggested, "It's a complex labyrinth. But one day it will be easy" (2011b, 7), licensing options continue to proliferate and many of these kinds of decisions will likely be with us for the near future. The American Library Association has released *Ebook Business Models: A Scorecard for Public Libraries* (2013), which outlines the types of questions librarians should consider when purchasing an e-book plan. These questions relate to the number of simultaneous users, ownership of content, and ease of integration with the library's catalog. While e-book business models are rapidly changing, many of the questions facing all types of libraries will continue to be about access.

Cathy Leverkus and Shannon Acedo (2013) have discussed many of these issues as they apply to school libraries; these authors gathered very specific details about current vendors, devices, acquisition plans, and publisher restrictions on e-books.

The intent of the following discussion is to distill some of the decisions facing school librarians to some of the basic questions about e-book acquisitions that will likely persist for the near future. The following discussion examines these questions as they relate to a single title. How long will the library have access to this title and what kinds of user-access to the title are available? The answers to these questions may have different associated costs.

HOW LONG WILL LEARNERS HAVE ACCESS?

When a school library purchases an e-book from a vendor, how long will the school library have access to that e-book? A factor related to this question is the library's dependence on the vendor because the book will be downloaded or streamed from the vendor's delivery platform to devices.

Some plans will allow the library access to the title for a specified term and that access must be renewed every year (or after a preset number of years), depending on the plan. Some publishers have implemented licenses that require repurchase of the book after a certain number of circulations (Bishop and Visser 2013). Other plans allow the library to "own" the item indefinitely through **perpetual access**, but this access may be dependent on an ongoing relationship with the vendor that might endure only as long as annual hosting fees are paid. If the library changes to another vendor, access to titles "bought" from the previous vendor may be lost. This issue came to the attention of librarians through the public librarians' experience with Overdrive, an early provider of e-content for libraries (Russell 2012).

These questions about subscription terms and future access are not new for libraries, but they make ownership of print books look comparatively straight-forward and attractive to schools where, year-to-year, budgets are often at risk.

At Champion High School, as John considers adding e-books to the collection he is faced with various models of e-book purchases. Two in particular interest him. The first is the concept of **patron-driven acquisitions** *that would allow a student or staff member who needs an item to access it immediately; the school would be billed for the purchase at the time of access. A faculty member has asked John and his principal to think about exploring this model on a limited basis—perhaps starting with faculty requests or allowing purchases-on-demand from a limited set of titles—with an annual cap so that the school can budget for the amount. John points out that currently the school library can request such* items in print editions through interlibrary loan at no cost and generally receive the item within a day or two.

The second model of interest looks like a "rent to own" option similar to the patron-driven model. After a predetermined number of uses, the school would automatically purchase and be billed for the item (Morris and Sibert 2011, 105).

These models are attractive because they can provide one-time access to specialized titles at a lower cost than purchase. Committing to either model will be a challenging budget problem requiring the teachers and librarian to make a projection about potential demand. John reminds his principal that the purchase of a hardcover book represents a similar gamble since the book might see little or no use despite the funds applied to its purchase.

Many of us have the print book long-term ownership model in mind as we shop for e-book plans, but the short-term lease models for e-books have benefits as well. Several authors have suggested the benefits of short-term lease as a model for schools; multiple users have access to an e-book for a limited time period while a class or grade is studying a topic or piece of literature (Foote 2013; Harris 2013). The purchase-on-demand or rental models have the advantage that the library will not pay for the item until it is actually needed by a patron. The purchase-on-demand model can potentially remove the job of selection from the school librarian. Perhaps we could have options that allowed selections to be constrained to certain databases or sets that have met selection criteria set by the librarian in collaboration with a library advisory committee. Alternatively, e-books requested by patrons could be submitted for some expedited method of approval based on pre-established, documented criteria. Patron-driven acquisitions is a model that has been explored by several academic libraries (see, for example, Fischer et al. 2012) and recommended for school libraries (Foote 2013).

E-BOOK SETS

Some e-book plans feature subscriptions to sets or bundled collections of e-book titles (Sanborn 2011). These sets offer ease of selection and, sometimes, a break in costs compared with purchasing individual titles. To determine the cost effectiveness of these plans, school librarians must consider how much of the set is needed and whether the items in the set are available individually. Sets are attractive for system-wide consortia selection, especially if the resources have been selected to represent a core collection of interest and need across various schools.

Of course, books selected for every school will not meet every need of individual schools. Such collections may help to jump start individual schools into making e-books available to students; however, these sets should be supplemented with local selections to meet local needs and interests identified for individual school communities.

QUESTIONS ABOUT MULTIPLE-USER ACCESS

A potential advantage of an electronic book is that users are not limited to one-at-a time access. When a print book is checked out, it's not available for any other reader. Libraries purchase multiple copies of high-demand books to meet this need. Depending on licensing, e-books can be available to a specified number of simultaneous users or to an unlimited number. If unlimited access is available and purchased, a library or a school system would only ever have to purchase one copy of a book, and everyone who had password access to the catalog could read the book whenever they wanted to. This is clearly a model that's unsustainable for many vendors or publishers unless the cost is set very high. Purchase plans for e-books reflect this access and cost reality.

One approach, the **single-user model**, allows a library to "loan out" an e-book title to only one user at a time, paralleling access to a traditional print book. Libraries can purchase multiple copies of e-books, just as they can for physical books, to allow multiple users access to the title. This is a model that's easily understood by librarians and by patrons, but it fails to leverage the electronic advantage of unlimited multiple users.

Another model **unlimited user model** allows for unlimited simultaneous readers generally for a much higher cost; in fact the cost would be prohibitive if applied to the entire collection. The only restriction placed on the use of these titles is the need for a login account and a password. For some titles, paying the price for this unlimited use makes sense when the per-use cost is considered—especially for a book that will be required reading for a whole grade in a school or school system.

In between single-user and unlimited access are multiple-user licensing models that limit the quantity of simultaneous users or provide unlimited access for a specified period of time. One or more of these models might be appealing in a school where some titles will be whole-class, small group, or book club selections.

For the near future, school librarians will likely continue to face this menu of choices for many of the titles they are considering for purchase. Carolyn Morris and Lisa Sibert (2011) discuss several of these options related to e-book acquisitions. Other issues to consider in addition to these business models include content and functionality. Mirela Roncevic (2013) also offers a thorough outline of these considerations. While the field will likely continue to evolve, the questions about how to select and provide access to the specific titles needed to meet the needs and interests of specific patrons will persist. Educators have particular interests in electronic textbooks and e-books for group and classroom use in addition to titles needed for individual use. School librarians will find unique challenges and opportunities in selection and acquisitions to meet those needs.

WHAT ABOUT FREE E-BOOKS?

John, the librarian at Champion high school, has also recognized the availability of materials, including e-books, on the "free Web" and has begun to publicize and link to these materials. Identifying, selecting, providing access and sustaining access to these materials requires training and time. While he recognizes that these materials are not truly "free," he sees a huge resource for English classes studying classic literature and for students to gain access through their smartphones and other devices.

The same types of questions should be applied to the selection of free materials as to more costly materials including the authority, merit, ease of use, and value to the collection. Free may have hidden costs, and the school librarian can help the school community evaluate a resource and its true cost over time. School librarians need staffing and time to identify quality free resources, as well as time to update and maintain such collections. Some resources offer free limited access to promote purchase, or they include advertisements that may be distracting. Free resources may be unstable over time. Businesses may be bought out by another company that decides to charge for access, or resources may simply disappear overnight.

DEVICE QUESTIONS

E-book acquisitions, whether free or purchased, require devices for access. Various purchase models and vendors need to be scrutinized for compatibility with patron or school-owned devices. In many cases, schools may already own sets of tablets or laptops and will want to consider their compatibility with various e-book plans. Increasingly students will want to access e-books through their own devices such as smartphones, tablets, or e-readers and school libraries will want to consider plans that are device-neutral. Collection development plans for e-books should address the need to purchase e-readers or other devices that students can check-out.

Currently, three different methods of delivery for e-book content are of interest to school librarians. An early model was to circulate e-readers with a preloaded selection of e-books. The legality of this model has been questioned, particularly when a single purchase was loaded on multiple devices. Leverkus and Acedo (2013, 70) caution that libraries must purchase one copy of each book if the plan is to circulate devices with preloaded titles.

A second model has been implemented in many public libraries. Patrons use their own devices and their library cards to download e-book titles to their devices for a limited circulation period. This model has its challenges, given the variety of devices owned by patrons and the need to educate each patron specific to the device owned. Equity will also be an issue if some patrons lack their own devices.

In a third model, particularly applicable to schools, content is streamed to a device that is connected to the Internet. These titles will be well suited for desktop computers and tablets because the resources will require access to a network to view. A student won't be able to walk out of the school and still read these titles on the school bus or at home unless in the presence of Internet service. If the network is down or slow, access may be interrupted or impaired.

In each of these models, the ownership or access to the e-book is separate from the ownership of the device. As multiple e-books can be downloaded and read on a single device, the per-use cost of the device becomes less significant. Additionally, if a device is lost or damaged, any e-book previously loaded to the device can be loaded or streamed to another device. Consider the purchase of an individual e-book downloaded to a device. The device itself requires an investment, yet the book is probably priced less than a hardcover and closer to the cost of a paperback. If anything happens to the evice, the right to the library's access to the e-book still endures, and it can be downloaded to another device. As multiple e-books can be downloaded on a device, the cost of the device becomes less significant. Still, school librarians must address the question of devices. What devices will students and classrooms need to access e-books?

Einstein Middle School was one of the first schools to experiment with e-books and purchased a set of e-readers preloaded with e-books. Over time, however, the school library program was locked into using the brand of e-reader originally purchased. While the library "owned" the license to titles on these devices, this ownership was meaningless for other brands of e-readers. This experience has led Jean to look for e-book plans through which titles can be downloaded and read on any e-reader or other device with an e-reader app. Jean has created mini-tutorials available from the library's website about how to download titles to different devices.

Like Einstein, most school libraries will want to look for e-book plans that allow titles to be read on the wide variety of devices owned by students and their families. Even with the proliferation of student-owned devices, schools should budget for and purchase some sort of device for classrooms and individuals. Instructional advantages may be evident when everyone in a class is using the same type of device; all readers can locate specific paragraphs easily and use common features like the dictionary or highlighting.

The cost of e-readers has lowered significantly; the least expensive now cost about as much as a reference book. Some librarians are still reluctant, though, to circulate e-readers because of replacement cost. However, librarians who are contemplating the circulation of e-readers that are pre-loaded with content should consider that ownership or access to the e-books will not be lost if the e-reader is lost or damaged. Given these cost considerations, school librarians could consider circulation of devices to students on a basis similar to the circulation policy for hardcover books.

ACCESS: WHAT COUNTS

The introduction of e-books to our collections clearly offers new challenges to school libraries. Acquisitions and licenses provide a current challenge, but the shift to electronic formats brings attention to other core issues of libraries.

The mission of school libraries to "ensure that students and staff are effective users of ideas and information" is wholly dependent on access to ideas and information. While libraries have long been associated with books, they are fundamentally about access to the ideas and information contained in those books and other formats. E-books and electronic databases offer new formats that extend some kinds of access while restricting others. A wise collection development plan must consider the needs of our students and the potential divide created by the technology needed to access e-books. In the past, we were able to count the volumes on our shelves and their circulations among our patrons as evidence that we were providing access. Electronic formats don't have the same visibility in our collections or offer our patrons the same kind of access. These new formats should cause us to question whether the quantitative standards we used in the past were ever a sufficient measure of what really counts: the ability of all users to access ideas and information.

GLOSSARY OF BOLD TERMS

license—A contract between the library and publisher, vendor, or producer that outlines rights and limitations on access to content.

multiple user model—A type of e-book license that allows more than one person to have access to an e-book at the same time. Multiple-user licenses are limited to a pre-set number of users.

patron-driven acquisitions—A business model that allows patrons to gain immediate access to a desired title; the library is then billed for the acquisition (Fischer et al. 2013).

perpetual access—A type of e-book license that grants a library continued future access to a title. While this model looks like ownership, librarians must read the fine print as access may be dependent on a continuing relationship with the provider and may require annual fees (Russell 2012).

short-term lease—A business model that allows the library access to a title for a short time period (Harris 2013). This model may be attractive at schools where access to a title for classroom use is needed, especially if the lease permits multiple simultaneous users.

single-user model—A type of e-book license that allows only one patron at a time to have access to the title. This model resembles the print book that is checked out to one person at a time for a restricted time period. Libraries may purchase multiple copies of these titles (similar to how libraries handled high demand for print titles).

Subscription—A business model that is very familiar to librarians. The library has access to digital content on an annual (or other time frame) basis with recurring fees to sustain access.

Unlimited user model—a type of e-book license that allows an unlimited number of simultaneous users.

REFLECTIVE QUESTIONS

▶ What are the ramifications of vendor/publisher ownership of our library books—in particular, related to vendors' ability to change or censor content after access has been purchased?

▶ What types of devices could be purchased to provide access to all students and how will those devices circulate?

▶ What combination of e-book plans is best for our school?

▶ Will the e-book vendor supply circulation data about the e-books in our collection?

▶ Will e-book vendors maintain students' privacy?

▶ Can individual e-books be "weeded" from the collection?

▶ How will I deal with a challenge to an e-book?

Chapter 8

Counting on What We Have: Evaluating Collections

GENERAL EVALUATION RELATED TO NEEDS ASSESSMENT

What should we count and what can our students count on? In chapter 3, a needs assessment was defined as a process to identify the gap between a desired state and an actual state, in this case, of the library collection. An important aspect of this needs assessment is the evaluation of the current collection. In fact, it's the aspect of needs assessment that drives a cycle of continuous improvement. We evaluate what we have and make changes to reach a desired goal. Then we again evaluate what we have for the purposes of measuring the effectiveness of those changes and identifying remaining gaps. In this chapter we look in more depth at measures of our collections that might serve this continuous cycle of improvement focused on access and learning.

Early school library standards specified quantitative collection measures and advocated ratios related to the school's enrollment. For many people, a rule of thumb was that a school library needed to have at least ten books per student and budgets should allocate funds to add at least one book per year per student. These standards even specified the number of inches of shelving and the square feet of space in the school library to maintain a "correct" ratio with the number of students. Measures were added about the currency of the collection, and automation facilitated calculating collection age and targeting particular sections of the collection, such as the 500s to measure support for the science curriculum. Circulation statistics added another measure of the use of the collection or a section of the collection.

Quantitative standards were useful measures that carried weight with funding and accreditation bodies in the past, but those measures said very little about the quality, the kinds of materials in those collections, who had access to them, or how they were used. These standards were one-size-fits-all measures that failed to address local contexts, such as demographics, teacher styles, or the varying characteristics of students, families, and communities. Two schools might appear very similar in terms of enrollment, grade levels, and curricula yet require very different kinds of library resources. Quantitative standards were especially silent about what kinds of learning happened in those library spaces and with those resources.

In 1998 the American Association of School Librarians and the Association for Educational Communications and Technology marked an important shift in the school library profession with the publication of *Information Power: Building Partnerships for Learning* and the inclusion of information-literacy standards for students. Then in 2007 AASL released *Standards for the 21st-Century Learner* as a freely available document, separate from the program guidelines. These new learning standards shifted the emphasis in school libraries to student learning, rather than focusing on what the library owned or the library's physical space.

This promulgation of learning standards marks a significant shift that calls for a similar shift in evaluative measures of the library's collection that move away from what is owned to what is accessible for learning. Collections that are locked up the minute buses arrive for dismissal, on weekends, and for months during the summer might be of the highest quality, quantity, and currency but their inaccessibility becomes a significant barrier to student learning. Generations of media formats came and went without students ever having direct access to them. Videocassettes may have counted as part of a school library's collection, but no student was ever allowed to check these out. Shelves of materials that no one uses might look adequate, but they aren't. Digital formats promise access beyond the library's hours, but students without access to required devices or networks will be closed out.

KINDS OF COLLECTION EVALUATION

Over the years, Champion High School has developed a reputation for an exemplary print collection. When John started at the school he discovered shelves bulging with books that provided the apparent quantity of resources needed to meet departmental and student needs. However, upon close investigation John realized that the average age of the books in the collection was old. He began a systematic evaluation of the collection looking at the age, circulation statistics, and relevance for each title. As a result of this evaluation he launched a major weeding effort. He used the data from this evaluation plus teachers' dissatisfaction with the existing collection to advocate and receive budget funds to purchase newer titles for the collection.

Fiction presented a unique challenge since the classics, while needed, were older and circulated less than the more-popular, high-demand titles read by students. Over the years, John also attended to the fiction collection with close attention to new trends and reviews of new fiction. The Champion PTA was pleased to support the development of this section, and it was soon recognized as an exemplary selection focused on the broad interests and needs of high school students. But in recent years John has noticed circulation and demand for this section of the library has fallen off; he wonders about how he might provide better access. Should he genre-fy this part of the collection? Does he need to increase the e-book fiction selection?

John picks a week of the year and surveys every student who comes in to browse the fiction section during the week. The survey asks students to list what they were looking for and what they found. Each survey includes a space for further comments. Using this measure, John learns that students are often frustrated to find that all copies of high-demand titles are checked out. Additionally, several students come in looking for a specific genre, such as romance or science fiction, and are frustrated because they didn't know the authors to look for when browsing. He discovers that many students leave without the desired genre. He uses this data, along with the notes added by students asking for more e-books, to argue for purchasing e-book copies of popular fiction and to genre-fy part of the fiction collection to highlight high-interest genres beginning with those identified in the survey data.

NEED FOR MEASURES THAT EMPHASIZE ACCESS— OUTPUT MEASURES

John has recognized that a stronger measure of his collection takes into account the users of his collection, in this case: the students. Frances Bryant Bradburn described several such measures in her book *Output Measures for School Library Media Programs*. John has used the measure of the independent reading/informational fill rate, a measure that requires sampling students who come to the library during one week looking for materials independent of course requirements. This measure involves surveying or interviewing students who are browsing the library collection for materials for their personal reading or informational interests beyond class assignments. The surveys should be given during a typical week in the school year and involve asking each student to record what he or she came in looking for and whether or not the resource was found. Inclusion of an open-ended question asking for suggestions is also helpful.

The fill rate is determined by dividing the actual number of items found by the number of needed items. If a student is looking for *Jane Eyre* and finds two copies on the shelf, the fill rate would be 200 percent, but a student looking for a popular vampire book who finds that two of the library copies are checked out and another cannot be located on the shelf would result in a 0 percent fill rate.

Statistics developed from the aggregate of these surveys begin to tell a story. The more students included in the survey, the more robust this measure becomes. A school librarian may ask for parent or community volunteers to help collect this data over two one-week periods in a school year. Older students can complete the survey themselves, but volunteers can help to elicit responses from all students before they walk out.

COLLECTION MAPPING

Collection mapping is a broad term used to describe a holistic process of viewing the entire collection or a part of the collection. Most circulation systems allow the librarian to get a picture of the collection by call number; this report includes basic data about the number of titles in each section, their average age, and the number of circulations in a particular time period. This information is generally easy to collect and easy to share. Combined with enrollment numbers, these numbers will allow a quick snapshot of how many titles are available per student and how many circulations per student. Low numbers of titles per student may signal the need for more titles. Low numbers of circulation may be troubling as well, and deserve further attention to the access students have to the collection and other factors related to student use of the materials. These numbers really offer little information by themselves. High numbers of titles tell the librarian nothing about their quality, and high circulations don't indicate what is being read. Circulation numbers are also easy to inflate.

In-depth collection mapping is more effectively completed through the close examination of a section of the collection, or in the case of a large section like biography or fiction, a sample of the section. For example, a school librarian who wants to evaluate the biography section might look at every tenth or twentieth title and collect information of interest. An example is the types of diversity reflected by the ethnicity, gender, or currency of the biography subjects. The surprising fact, for example, that students browsing the biography collection are 83 percent more likely to find dead white men becomes a telling statistic.

Such statistics can be used to tell a story to argue for updating the collection with new funding and resources. Collection mapping is often used to map the library's resources with curriculum standards to determine the collection's potential to meet curricular needs. For example, the school library resources available to meet a grade-level goal in social studies might be identified and evaluated. This more-detailed collection mapping can be time-consuming, and school librarians often rotate through sections with a focus on one part of the collection every year.

As Sarah plans for an opening collection at Clarke Elementary, she will be faced with the question about how many titles she needs to purchase. Her system has provided the school with a budget based on quantitative benchmarks from similar school openings based on projected enrollments. But Sarah recognizes that enrollment numbers are only part of the consideration; also needed are adequate numbers of materials for different stages of readers, to meet curriculum for each grade level, and to reflect the varied interests of her community of readers. Her professional judgment will apply to the distribution of the budget in the selection of the actual titles and formats for the opening collection.

She will use a form of collection mapping to project some of the need. In particular, the state has just released a new science curriculum to be implemented in the upcoming year. Sarah uses the curriculum to identify areas of potential need and select items appropriate to both the content and grade level for each science goal. Even with this attention to the curriculum, Sarah's selections may be limited by what's available at the time as well as a budget that must be stretched across all curricular and student needs and interests. The truth about many opening collections is that, while everything in the library will be new, the opening collection won't have everything.

Some things will be immediately obvious the first time someone comes in and asks for a book about New Zealand or a biography of a contemporary sports figure. The first year, Sarah will need to evaluate the collection and how it is actually used by her students and teachers. She will likely encounter various "holes" in the collection and will be forced to justify a budget because of the perception that a new library has everything it needs. Sarah plans to implement an evaluation during the first half of the school year.

MEASURING STUDENT ACCESS

Given a focus on student access to materials needed for learning, the strongest measures for evaluating a collection take a combined look at the available titles in the collection, the curriculum, and the students who will be using the collection. Table 10 shows two such measures adapted from Bradburn's *Output Measures for School Library Media Programs.*

The "potential curriculum support rate" begins with a curriculum goal such as a science standard and examines the numbers of items in the collection that could potentially meet that standard. Identifying the items can be done in a very cursory way: taking the corresponding Dewey number and looking at the quantity of titles to make a value judgment of the adequacy. But an assessment of the potential curriculum support rate should really look across the collection at all kinds of materials, going beyond related Dewey numbers to include fiction, biography, and poetry, as well as audiovisual ma-

Table 10. Applying fill rate formula (Bradburn 1999).

Measure	Description	How to Calculate the Rate
Potential Curriculum Support Rate	Extent to which the collection will support a potential unit of instruction/curriculum needs.	Divide number of items that support the unit by the number of items needed for the unit (based on number of students simultaneously working on unit).
Curriculum Support Fill Rate	Extent to which the collection supports actual curriculum needs of teachers and students.	Divide the actual number of appropriate items available at the time of need that support an expressed need by the number of items needed by the teacher or student.

terials, online periodical databases, online reference tools, and other digital resources.

Because each standard is for a particular grade level, a further step involves examining the materials for appropriateness to the developmental level and intellectual and reading ability of the range of students in that grade level. This process is very time-consuming. However, an added value is the creation of lists of appropriate resources; these lists can be made available and searchable by teachers and students. When the school librarian collaborates with teachers to plan this particular unit, the list becomes a major source of information and value. Bradburn's potential curriculum support rate would divide the number of resources by the projected number of students who will need to use those resources. These values could then be compared to an established ideal number of resources such as two print titles per student for an elementary unit, or for older students one electronic book that could be streamed to all classroom computers simultaneously.

The potential curriculum support rate is a valuable measure that takes into account the curriculum, the resources owned by the library or school, and the projected numbers of students. But this rate represents an ideal. In actual practice, there may be factors that intervene to reduce the actual curriculum support fill rate. Items may be checked out or missing from the collection. Some titles may be available, but individuals lack the devices or equipment needed to use them. Individual students may be unable to access the materials that are most appealing or most appropriate to their individual learning needs or differences. The actual curriculum support fill rate is a stronger measure of student and teacher access to needed curriculum materials at the actual time of need.

Sarah hopes to open with a print collection that supports the new science curriculum, but she may not be able to order the sheer numbers needed to meet the demand based on projected enrollments, especially because her collection must meet other curricular and student interests. Sarah decides that she will choose a week during the school year to examine each science unit that is currently taught in each classroom and look particularly at the actual curriculum support fill rates for that particular week. This data will provide her with a snapshot of the school's science needs.

She shares these plans with the leadership team for the new school and members rally around the science theme, deciding to adopt a related focus for the new school. They plan a school-wide focus on the environment that will include recycling, a garden on campus, and other grade-level projects, including several themed parent nights. Excited about opening a new school with a shared focus, teachers offer to help Sarah recruit parent volunteers and participate in the week-long survey.

The school librarian and teachers might actually conduct this evaluation a week or two before the anticipated instruction. Given the planned goals and objectives for an upcoming week, the school librarian identifies and pulls together everything in the collection related to the topic. Materials should include and be separated into print, audiovisuals, electronic books, and periodical and reference databases. Teachers would then examine the selected materials and determine which ones they will directly use for instruction as well as the additional materials they would like to have available for students to use independently.

Each of these calculations might be mediated or complicated by local contexts (see table 11). If the teachers on a grade level decide to stagger the times when they will need a single-user item, one copy may be sufficient to meet the need. For example, a grade level may decide to pass a fifteen-minute DVD from classroom to classroom over a day or a couple of days. If an item is meant to be shared with a classroom of students as part of face-to-face instruction perhaps by projecting it to a whiteboard, then the rate can be calculated by the number of classrooms. However, if the teacher wants every student in the classroom to use the item, then the rate will be dependent on the number of users divided by the number of available devices. In a 1:1 environment the

Table 11. Calculating curriculum support fill rates for single-user and multiple-simultaneous-user items.

	Rate Calculation	Example Calculated with Six Classrooms per Grade Level in an Elementary School
Single-user items needed by all teachers on the grade level for face-to-face whole class instruction.	Divide the number of copies of the item by the number of classrooms.	4 copies/6 classrooms = 67% 1 copy/6 classrooms = 17% 8 copies/6 classrooms = 100%
Multiple-simultaneous user items needed by all teachers on the grade level for instruction.	Divide the number of simultaneous users by the number of classrooms.	5 simultaneous users/6 classrooms = 83% 12 simultaneous users/6 classrooms = 100% Unlimited users/6 classrooms = 100%
Additional single-user items.	Divide the total number of additional items by the total number of students on the grade level.	35 items/140 students = 25%
Multiple simultaneous use electronic items for additional student use.	For each item, divide the number of available devices for student use by the total number of students per grade level.	36 devices (12 classroom computers and a set of 24 tablets)/140 students = 26%

need for devices is a non-issue, and the rate will be dependent of the number of simultaneous users allowed divided by the actual number of students who need to use the item. This measure may be especially important in a BYOD environment where not all student-owned devices may be equipped to access the item. In this case the calculation for an item with unlimited simultaneous use would be the number of devices that can access the item divided by the number of students. In a classroom of twenty-six students, where twenty students have an appropriate device, the fill rate is 77 percent. This fill rate might be mediated by school-owned devices available at the time.

The consistent calculation and recording of this fill rate based on the number of appropriate and available devices at the time of student need will highlight the cost-effectiveness of purchasing devices for student use. Schools will not be seeing the full use of online periodical databases, encyclopedias, or multiple-user electronic books if students do not have enough devices to access those items. Similarly, out-of-school use of licensed electronic resources will be at a lower rate based on student access to devices or networks needed to access those materials.

The real question of student access is best calculated with an individual fill rate similar to the one John used to evaluate his fiction collection. Individual students could be asked how many items they needed to meet a homework assignment, or a project requiring out-of-school work and how many items they actually were able to access. For example, one student, Sally, had a project that required an encyclopedia, two magazine articles, and three books to complete. Her family does not have Internet access so she was not able to access the online encyclopedia or periodical database. One of the books was available as an electronic book, and she was able to download that to her cell phone. Sally needed six items for the project and was able to access the three needed books. The individual fill rate for Sally is 50 percent. Even in a large, affluent school, there may be a hundred Sallys whose learning needs are only half met, and these learners are multiplied by numerous nights of homework. Compound this with Sally's limited access to leisure reading in e-book format, and the loss is staggering. This reduced access to resources will be the price some students' will pay for the shift in collections to electronic formats—unless school librarians find ways to provide devices and Internet access beyond the school day and the school walls.

Similar measures can be applied to equipment and other tools, library space, or even infrastructure elements such as power outlets or the capacity of the wireless network for multiple simultaneous users. Snapshots of actual class sessions may reveal that even under seemingly ideal conditions with devices and resources, if students experience difficulty with a particular resource, the actual rate may be considerably less than the potential fill rate. For example the number of successful Internet or database searches will likely result in a lower actual fill rate than the potential support rate. These fill rates might provide a rationale for targeted instruction and/or for a collection of appropriate websites. Information searches limited by the time needed to search multiple databases, the library catalog, and the Web might justify the acquisition of more sophisticated federated search tools that allow a patron to simultaneously search multiple databases.

At Einstein Middle School, Jean decides to try mapping the collection to AASL's Standards for the 21st-Century Learner (2007). As she talks with teachers they decide to measure the standard: "Use technology and other information tools to organize and display knowledge and understanding in ways that others can view, use, and assess" (3.1.4). The eighth-grade team decides to examine the digital storytelling projects completed by small groups for the social studies unit on the Harlem Renaissance. Jean breaks the standard down to look at the collection for tools for organizing information, tools for displaying knowledge, and tools for sharing knowledge with others. Every group will have access to a tablet equipped with a camera and app for capturing video, and she uses her knowledge of the project to select and acquire an app for storyboarding, and a choice of apps for creating a digital storytelling product. The potential fill rate looks like 100 percent for the twenty small groups from the grade level.

However, when the project is actually implemented the fill rate is decreased because one device was not charged and two devices were too full for new video files. The actual fill rate for this class session is closer to 85 percent. Five groups are frustrated in their initial search for the still images they want for their projects so this fill rate falls to 75 percent. A sound-editing app is not available, and Jean adds this to a list of desired apps for purchase. Students want to share their completed videos on a video-sharing site but are blocked by the school filter; in this case the actual fill rate is zero percent. Four groups are unable to complete their project within the time allotted and must find other times when they can work. In this case the time allotted to work in the library space meets 80 percent of the need. One group needs additional assistance from the librarian and is unable to schedule time during the school day. The fill rate for expert assistance is 95 percent.

Following each library session, Jean asks students to complete a quick survey about their access to the tools they needed for their group projects. She learns that some of the students have had experience with another, more costly video-editing app and were often frustrated by the constraints of the ones available on the tablets. The fill rate to meet their perceived needs looks more like 80 percent. Several also commented on difficulty getting around the school filters to find the images or music they wanted to use with their projects. Two groups comment that they were unable to access a quiet space for their audio recording. As Jean reads over the student surveys, she realizes there were some materials that students might have found in the print collection, and she is reminded that library resources don't count if students are not aware of their existence.

WEEDING THE COLLECTION

Any in-depth examination of the collection, such as collection mapping or a fill-rate survey, will likely uncover titles that are no longer current, appealing, or relevant. These titles, along with materials that are falling apart or otherwise in disrepair, should be evaluated for removal from the collection. As John discovered when he came to Champion, items such as these outdated or worn-out print items provide a false sense of the potential fill rates. Copyright dates and circulation statistics offer some guidance about potential titles that should be weeded, but an actual examination of the item in the context of other materials available in the collection is preferred. An item that has not circulated may have been overlooked because of it's appearance or classification in the collection; therefore, it may need to be promoted through displays or conversations with students and teachers. Weeding decisions should also be made about formats and equipment that are no longer used.

COUNT ON LEARNING

Student learning and student access to the materials and resources needed for learning are what count in each of these scenarios. We can't afford to count items that are not being used because there is not sufficient equipment, or items are locked in a closet because we are fearful they will be broken or lost. Even inexpensive items or free items that took time to acquire come at too high of a cost if they are never used. The more an item is used, the more the per-use cost is lowered. Quantitative standards may set minimal benchmarks; they are useful figures for the opening of a new school for example, but they are not sufficient.

Today's school settings further complicate efforts to count, because an electronic item may be used simultaneously by every student in the school and yet, some students may never be able to use that item beyond the school day and outside the school network. How do we count these items? We need more-nuanced measures that take into account issues of access as well as actual use by students and teachers.

In each of the scenarios in this chapter, the collection of data is important but meaningless unless it is shared with others. Part of the collection in each scenario is invisible, and it's the job of the school librarian to make it visible.

Actual fill rates for e-books, apps, and subscription databases show the value and use of these collections. In the middle school example, high fill rates are evidence of the value and use of the tablets and the apps loaded on them. They also highlight issues of access beyond the materials, including factors such as devices, filters, time, expertise, and space. Direct surveys of students and teachers allow the librarian to share the voices of those directly impacted by budget decisions. The library budget is not about the library or the librarian; it's about the students in the school and their learning. Other kinds of measures, including numbers of titles and circulations, allow us to measure what we have. Fill rates allow us to measure what's missing from the collection; these measures help us identify gaps and assess needs to inform future collection decisions and budgets.

Many of the measures suggested in this chapter are costly in terms of the time they will take. School librarians are encouraged to elicit help from teachers, parents, and other volunteers from the school community. Such requests will further public relations for the school library and underscore the library's learning focus on student needs and interests. These measures are best done as part of a long-range plan that examines a manageable part of the collection each year. In turn, results of these measures should be shared broadly. These measures make the collection and, more importantly, access to the collection more clearly visible than orderly shelves of books ever did.

REFLECTIVE QUESTIONS

▶ Has our school recently adopted new state or national standards? What areas of the collection need attention to support these standards?

▶ What areas of our collection are of particular concern right now? What measures could I apply to those areas?

▶ What was a unit for which I recently collaborated with teachers to plan? What types of resources were available to support that unit? What additional resources would enhance the lesson the next time it is taught?

Chapter 9

Collection Development: A Plan for Continuous Improvement

The purpose of developing and maintaining a library's collection is not the collection itself but the collection as a means to meet the needs of students and staff for up-to-date, accessible and relevant materials of the highest quality in support of enacting the school's curriculum goals. Collection development is an ongoing process that never ends; evaluation drives the cycle of continuous improvement as needs are identified for the next phase. Providing and evaluating access to the resources in the collection are also key drivers of the process. Questions raised about access may suggest the need for more resources or may highlight the need for new procedures or updated infrastructure to support access.

How do we pull together all the elements of the cycle depicted in figure 5? One of the most effective means to communicate and implement the process is through the development and dissemination of a written collection-development plan. Creating and following a written plan forces us to slow down to look holistically at our library programs and resources. Guiding statements about

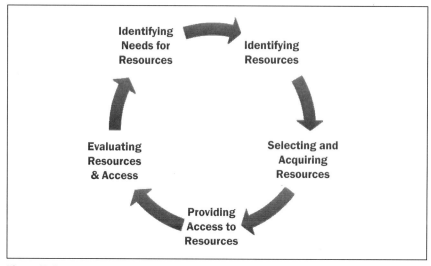

Figure 5. Collection-development continuous-improvement cycle.

intellectual freedom, equity, and access along with the school's and school system's mission statements help to establish a context and rationale for the goals detailed in the plan. As goals and action steps to reach them are put in writing, a plan may reveal missing steps or issues that should be resolved. When a new technology is added, what are the long-term ramifications in terms of replacements, repairs, or needed infrastructure or storage? In the process of writing the plan, we may uncover questions we had overlooked about our school community, the library's resources, and how we will evaluate access to those resources. A written plan should include both long- and short-range goals. The short-range goals should include action steps to guide the process and ensure that nothing is overlooked. Involving stakeholders in the process of writing the plan may bring missing perspectives to the process. A written plan that prioritizes needs can be consulted as decisions are made, including decisions about using unforeseen budget windfalls or coping with shortfalls. The written plan could be shared in a wiki or other online document. This sharing would allow for updating and also provide links to other relevant documents, such as a school board selection policy or relevant AASL position statements and other ALA documents. The time and thought put into a written plan may also aid in the writing of grants.

A collection-development plan should include an overview of selection criteria and the selection process. School board policy regarding the selection of library materials as well as procedures for challenges to library materials should be included in the plan.

A written plan also becomes an important tool for public relations. Not everyone in the public will want to wade through the entire plan. The plan should include an executive summary that outlines the big picture, presents the budget, and demonstrates a focus on student learning and access. There may be a need to present the plan to a school's leadership team or PTA. While a collection-development plan may be a written document, other types of media might be used to share the plan by employing visuals and storytelling. Evaluation data from surveys and actual fill rates may tell a compelling story about the learning focus of the library and the concrete impacts of funding decisions. A wise collection-development plan is not in the school librarian's head; it has a form that can be consulted, evaluated, and shared.

During the first year, Sarah shares with teachers in each grade level the evaluation she has done for the potential fill rate for that grade level's science curriculum. Together they prioritize the need for more individual books. Doubling a selection might bring them from a 10 to a 20 percent fill rate, for example—not ideal, but twice as good. To meet the need for some content, they examine e-book sets that the publisher has targeted for this curriculum area and grade levels. While expensive, the cost divided among the number of potential simultaneous users looks like a good use of funds. They also have a wish list of models that will help to deliver the curriculum. As Sarah does this for each grade level, the numbers come together to create an ideal budget that she takes to the library advisory committee for approval and then to the leadership team. With input and support built from all of these stakeholders, the library budget is one of the first items approved for the next school year.

HOW IT ALL FITS TOGETHER

Building and developing a collection of library resources is an integral part of each of the roles of the school librarian addressed in *Empowering Learners*: leader, instructional partner, teacher, information specialist, and program administrator. As a teacher, the school librarian knows the students in the school and guides them to use information in a variety of formats. Working collaboratively with teachers, the school librarian helps to design instruction in the role of instructional partner. These teaching and collaborative relationships also enable the identification of resource needs that become part of a collection-development plan. As formats shift to more types of digital resources, the school librarian draws on expertise as an information specialist to identify, select, and evaluate technology, including devices and networks needed to access information in these formats. In the case of collection development all of these roles are significant but the roles of program administrator and leader are especially important to the development and dissemination of a collection-development plan. Such a plan requires the administrative skills of budgeting, selection, and acquisitions, but as a leader, the school librarian ensures that all stakeholders contribute and are aware of the process.

A written three- to five-year plan is an important tool in collection development. The plan should take into account the cycle of collection development with regular evaluation, identification of needed resources, selection and acquisition of those resources as the budget allows, followed by evaluation of the effectiveness of those resources and the further need for more resources. In this way the school library collection becomes a living part of the mission of the school that grows and is replenished in response to the learning needs of the school community. A written collection-development plan becomes a document that can guide decision making and careful use of budget resources.

The process of writing the plan requires attention to details, including a long-range assessment of needs, a forward projection to meet those needs, and careful thought about the big picture of the school community and of the collection. Written with input from stakeholders such as members of a library advisory committee, the written plan expresses the desires of the school community as a whole. The document can be shared with the entire school community but particularly with funding sources, including administrators and leadership teams but also community business partners or other potential grant sources. A written collection-development plan also provides accountability and allows for ongoing evaluation of how well goals were met.

WHAT SHOULD BE INCLUDED IN A COLLECTION-DEVELOPMENT PLAN

A plan for collection development should address the learning needs and interests of the community, the status of the current collection, identification of specific areas of concern, and a detailed plan including budget figures for addressing the needs in each area. Few, if any, school libraries have the resources to meet all needs at once. Even if the budget were unlimited, the careful evaluation and targeted attention of a collection require time and analysis to adequately complete. Even the carefully selected collection for the new school is a projection of anticipated needs that will likely not include everything—either because a need was not anticipated or an item was not available to fill a particular need, or simply because the school has to stretch resources to meet as many needs as possible with some unmet the first year.

One way to think about the collection is to divide it into three to five parts and create a plan to focus on each part in each of the next three to five years. One such plan for an elementary school used the Dewey Decimal Classification system to think about the collection as it related to major curriculum standards (see table 12). This plan might also provide a framework for other decisions, such as whom to invite for author visits or selection of a common read. Schools looking for an annual school-wide focus may follow the lead established by the library's collection-development plan to have a science focus one year, and then a social studies focus, followed by a reading focus.

Other plans might divide up attention to the collection through curriculum standards. In states where standards are revised on a regular cycle, a collection-development plan might synch with that cycle to ensure resources

Table 12. Sample collection-development plan focus for three-year plan.

Year One	Year Two	Year Three
• Science and Math	• Social Studies	• Literature and Arts
• Dewey 100s, 500s, 600s	• Dewey 200s, 300s, (including folklore) 900s, biography	• Dewey 400s, 700s, 800s
• fiction: science fiction, picture books related to science curriculum	• fiction: historical fiction, picture books related to social studies curriculum	• fiction: fantasy, realistic picture books
• science films, tools, models	• films, maps and globes	• audiobooks, films, art prints or slides, writing tools
Every Year		
• award-winning and notable titles		
• subscriptions to periodicals, databases, and e-books		
• all formats: audiobooks, videos, e-books, devices, graphic novels, etc.		

will be available to support new or revised standards. Another way to slice the plan would be by grade levels; this approach would provide a way of looking at how the collection supports the developmental or other grade-level-specific needs of students. An example is the needs of high school sophomores and juniors for information about colleges and career choices. A plan might also revisit specific formats regularly. For example graphic novels might be targeted every third year, or a technology like tablets would be re-evaluated at regular intervals for replacement or upgrade. However the plan divides the collection, the creators of the plan must attend to the big picture; the plan must be flexible enough to allow critical needs to be met, regardless of the year of the plan and to guide wise spending of unexpected or grant funds. In any given budget year, there may be more needs than funds. The annual plan will include priorities that fit projected funding. It's always wise to have a plan that exceeds projections. Principals remember that the school librarian will wisely spend unexpected funds that have to be allocated at the last minute.

ACTION STEPS

A collection-development plan should include a timeline outlining specific actions including evaluation and needs assessment, preparation of a detailed budget, plans for identification, selection, and purchasing of resources, and plans to publicize access to new materials.

John successfully presented his plan to grow the e-book collection, a plan that included purchasing devices for student checkout, and his projected budget was approved at a May leadership meeting. When John leaves in June, the e-book and device orders have been prepared and are ready to send when the new budget year begins. An important and ultimately time-saving task John did was the development of "wish lists" for items that he finds are well-reviewed and meet his long-range plans for the collection. John maintains these wish lists in a spreadsheet that includes price and other ordering information, the source of the review, and the areas of the collection and the collection-development plan addressed by the item. John can readily use this spreadsheet to create new orders as soon as funds are approved. The anticipated timeline for John's next school year looks like table 13.

The timeline in table 13 reflects the rhythm of a typical school budget year in which funds become available July 1. Often the principal and leadership team make budget decisions in May or June. A wise school librarian

Table 13. Sample action steps timelime.

Ongoing	Librarian maintains spreadsheet and "wish lists" based on reading reviews.
July 1	Orders submitted.
August	Orders received, checked in. New e-book list and procedures are shared at first faculty meeting and during student orientations.
October	One week selected for evaluation of e-books by means of individual fill rate measures.
January	STEM sections of the library are evaluated using the potential curriculum fill rate. In the process, items from part of the collection are examined, and weeding decisions are made.
February	One week selected for evaluation of STEM materials in collection using actual curriculum fill rates. Library advisory committee analyzes data from this and the previous evaluation to identify and prioritize collection needs. LAC also reviews long-range collection-development plan for other areas targeted for upcoming budget year.
March	Detailed budget, prepared to meet gaps found in STEM evaluation and other ongoing collection needs, is shared with LAC, principal, and leadership team. Detailed budget is framed with the overall three- to five-year collection-development plan.
April	Librarian uses files, selection tools, and reviews to identify specific items, costs, and vendors in preparation for ordering.
May	Principal and leadership team review all budget requests from the school including the library's detailed budget. Needs are prioritized, and funds are allocated. Based on collection priorities, the librarian adjusts orders to reflect actual allocated funds.
June	Following the end of the school year, the librarian leaves for a family vacation. Orders dated July 1 and signed by the principal are on file with the secretary.

anticipates this event by presenting a budget as early as March. Budget years are rarely typical however. Some years funds might not be available until September. In other years, the principal will discover funds that must be spent in a hurry in February or March. In either case, the school librarian who has a written plan with clear priorities and has a "wish list" that details potential purchases is in position to spend funds both wisely and quickly. In John's many years of experience, even in the most lean budget years, principals have funds that must be spent at the last minute or be lost, and John's principal knows that he can rely on John to recommend priorities that serve the entire school.

COMMUNICATION

Jean recognizes that communication is a key aspect of her collection-development plan. At Einstein Middle School, the school library's collection includes technology devices, apps, software, and equipment. In addition to meeting with her library advisory committee, the school's leadership team, and the PTA, Jean schedules regular appointments with her principal to sit down to discuss student access to technology. She comes to those meetings with a prioritized list of tools needed by the school. These range from small purchases like power strips to more expensive items like a high-speed color printer, or consumables such as ink and paper for student use. At each of these meetings, the principal identifies pockets of discretionary funding that might be used to meet various needs. Jean serves as one of the principal's listening posts for technology needs of the school, and he trusts her holistic and long-range understanding of those needs. A need for power strips might be critical yet easily overlooked. When Jean brings it to his attention, funds are immediately identified, and he asks her to prepare an order.

Just as collection development draws on every one of the roles of the school librarian—leader, instructional partner, teacher, information specialist, and program administrator—it also draws the school librarian into the overall mission and goals of the school, the school system, and the community. As Jean became concerned with collecting the tools needed for the types of student creations promoted in *Standards for the 21st-Century Learner*, she became engaged with the school's overall technology plan. The school librarian who puts student learning and access first becomes a trusted member of the school team. Formats may shift, but a focus on student learning and access anchors our work, allows for the identification of priorities, and justifies the application of funding and perhaps, most importantly, trust.

REFLECTIVE QUESTIONS

▶ What stakeholders are essential advisors in the development of our collection-development plan?

▶ What documents such as school board policies or school improvement plans need to be aligned with my collection-development plan?

▶ How should I disseminate the highlights of the collection-development plan and to what audiences?

▶ What are annual recurring costs that need to be included in my budget?

▶ What is a realistic three- to five-year way to divide the library collection for evaluation and new acquisitions?

Conclusion and Acknowledgments
Reader *See Also* Author

When you have followed the *see also* references back to your original search term you know you are finished. Well, maybe. Libraries have never been settled, quiet places for me. Their shelves are dynamic with undiscovered doors that I have yet to open. Once opened, a book, a database, or a video invites me to engage with the ideas, images, sensations, and feelings in a magical suspension of myself. Librarians help to create this magic as they select, collect, and organize these materials, these doors of discovery.

As I finish this book, I know that I am writing in a moment that will soon shift again. School libraries and librarians will continue to face new challenges as modes of education and means of searching for information, creating new knowledge, and communicating continue to emerge or fade away. But I am optimistic about the profession because I believe we stand on a foundation of quality and access that will endure the most seismic shifts. Formats may change, but formats are only important as doorways for access. In libraries, we believe that access should be as unfettered as possible for all individuals, and we strive to provide a selection of high-quality materials for the access of individuals who make up the communities we serve. Collection development must ultimately be about those users and their access.

In Appendix A you will find a list of further reading to follow this book, but I cannot begin to acknowledge the many authors and librarians who have influenced my thinking and passion for librarianship. A few deserve special mention. Lester Asheim was my professor in my first semester of library school and gave me the gift of seeing librarianship as a noble, idealistic, and spirited profession. My first professional position was working with Lois Winkel, then editor of *Elementary School Library Collection.* I cannot begin to name all of the things I learned in that office about education, children's literature, collections, and school librarianship—but most particularly about high standards. Thanks to Frances Bryant Bradburn, not only for permission to use her output measures, but for years of professional guidance and leadership. Gail Dickinson, who, until recently was in the office next-door to me, deserves credit for endless debates about the future of school libraries—especially about whether we have lost our ability to count or quantify our collections and circulations. Finally, I want to acknowledge the work of Kay Bishop, whom the profession has recently lost, for her comprehensive textbook about collection management that was recently published in a fifth edition.

Works Cited

American Association of School Librarians. 2007. "Standards for the 21st-Century Learner." <www.ala.org/aasl/sites/ala.org. aasl/files/content/guidelinesandstandards/ learningstandards/AASL_Learning_ Standards_2007.pdf> (accessed March 1, 2013).

———. 2009. *Empowering Learners: Guidelines for School Library Programs.* Chicago: ALA.

American Library Association. 2013. "Ebook Business Models: A Scorecard for Public Libraries." <www.districtdispatch.org/wp-content/uploads/2013/01/Ebook_Scorecard. pdf> (accessed September 21, 2013).

Asheim, Lester. 1979. "The Professional Decision." In *Background Readings in Building Library Collections*, 2nd ed., edited by Phyllis Van Orden and Edith B. Phillips, 9–18. Metuchen, NJ: Scarecrow.

Bacon, Beth. 2013a. "Ebooks Are Actually Not Books: Schools among First to Realize. <www. digitalbookworld.com/2013/ebooks-are-

actually-not-books-schools-among-first-to-realize> (accessed September 21, 2013).

———. 2013b. "Streaming Ebooks: A New Distribution Model for Schools." <www.digitalbookworld.com/2013/streaming-ebooks-a-new-distribution-model-for-schools> (accessed September 21, 2013).

Bishop, Chanitra and Mirijke Visser. 2013. "E-Books? So What's the Big Deal?" *Young Adult Library Services* 11 (3): 4–8.

Bishop, Kay. 2013. *Collection Program in Schools: Concepts and Practices*, 5th ed. Santa Barbara, CA: Libraries Unlimited.

Bradburn, Frances Bryant. 1999. *Output Measures for School Library Media Programs*. New York: Neal-Schuman.

Dresang, Eliza T. 1999. *Radical Change: Books for Youth in a Digital Age*. New York: H.W. Wilson.

Fischer, Karen S., et al. 2012. "Give 'em What They Want: A One-Year Study of Unmediated Patron-Driven Acquisition of E-books." *College and Research Libraries* 73 (5): 469–492.

Foote, Carolyn. 2013. "For Ebooks, the Future Is Now…Maybe." *Internet@ Schools* 20 (3): 26–27.

Harris, Christopher. 2013. "Ebooks 2013: New Leasing Models, Cheaper Devices, More Content." *School Library Journal* 59 (1): 16.

Kaufman, Roger A., and Fenwick W. English. 1979. *Needs Assessment: Concept and Application*. Englewood Cliffs, NJ; Educational Technology.

Klobas, Jane E. 1997. "The Methods of Action Research." *School Libraries Worldwide* 3 (2): 11–30.

Leverkus, Cathy, and Shannon Acedo. 2013. *Ebooks and the School Library Program: A Practical Guide for the School Librarian*. Chicago: ALA.

Morris, Carolyn, and Lisa Sibert. 2011 "Acquiring E-Books." In *No Shelf Required: E-books in Libraries* edited by Sue Polanka, 95–124. Chicago: ALA.

Polanka, Sue. 2011a. "A Guide to Ebook Purchasing: Advice from the Author of *No Shelf Required* on How to Flex Your Library's Purchasing Muscle." <www.americanlibrariesmagazine.org/article/guide-ebook-purchasing> (accessed October 23, 2013).

———. 2011b. "Purchasing E-books In Libraries: A Maze of Opportunities and Challenges." *Library Technology Reports*. 47 (8): 4–7.

———. 2013. "Ebook Access: Business Models for Subscription Services." *Online Searcher* 37 (2): 65–67.

Roncevic, Mirela. 2013. "Criteria for Purchasing E-Book Platforms." In *E-Book Platforms for Libraries*, by Mirela Roncevic. *Library Technology Reports* 49 (3): 10–13.

Ruggiero, Lucia. n.d. "Digital Books: Could They Make Censorship and 'Book Burning' Easier?" <www.digitalmeetsculture.net/article/digital-books-could-they-make-censorship-and-book-burning-easier> (accessed October 17, 2013).

Russell, Carrie. 2012. "Threats to Digital Lending: Does the Durability Of Ebooks Pose a Digital Danger to Libraries?" *American Libraries Ebooks Supplement* <www.americanlibrariesmagazine.org/article/threats-digital-lending> (accessed October 23, 2013).

Sanborn, Lura D. 2011. "Ebook Collections for High Schools." *School Library Monthly* 28 (1). <www.schoollibrarymonthly.com/articles/Sanford2011-v28n1p37.html> (accessed October 21, 2013).

Appendix A
Further Reading

Bishop, Kay. 2013. *The Collection Program in School: Concepts and Practices*, 5th ed. Santa Barbara, CA: Libraries Unlimited.

Bradburn, Frances Bryant. 1999. *Output Measures for School Library Media Programs*. New York: Neal-Schuman.

Colgrove, Tod. 2013. "Libraries as Makerspace." *Information Technology and Libraries* (March) 1–5.

Doll, Carol A., and Pam Petrick Barron. 2002. *Managing and Analyzing Your Collection: A Practical Guide for Small Libraries and School Library Media Centers*. Chicago: ALA.

Dresang, Eliza T. 1999. *Radical Change: Books for Youth in a Digital Age*. New York: H.W. Wilson.

Franklin, Pat, and Claire Gatrell Stephens. 2009. "Use Standards to Draw Curriculum Maps." *School Library Media Activities Monthly* 25 (9): 44–45.

Gustafson, Ellen. 2013. "Meeting Needs: Makerspaces and School Libraries." *School Library Monthly* 29 (8): 35–36.

Hallstrom, Janet. 2013. "Building It Together: Life as a Virtual School Librarian." *Library Media Connection* 31 (5): 22–23.

Howard, Jody K. 2010. "Information Specialist and Leader: Taking on Collection and Curriculum Mapping." *School Library Monthly* 27 (1): 35–37.

———. 2011. "Basic Selection Tools: 21st-Century Style." *School Library Monthly* 28 (3): 9–11.

K–12 Digital Decisions. 2013. "Purchase or Lease?: Options for School Library Ebook Acquisitions." <www.k12digitaldecisions.com/purchase-or-lease> (accessed October 18, 2013).

Leverkus, Cathy, and Shannon Acedo. 2013. *Ebooks and the School Library Program: A Practical Guide for the School Librarian.* Chicago: ALA.

Loertscher, David V., and Laura Wimberley. 2009. *Collection Development Using the Collection Mapping Technique: A Guide for Librarians.* San Jose, CA: Hi Willow.

McNair, Ellen. 2012. "Print to Digital: Opportunities for Choice." *Library Media Connection* 30 (6): 28–30.

Polanka, Sue. 2011. *No Shelf Required: E-Books in Libraries.* Chicago: ALA.

———. 2012. *No Shelf Required 2: Use and Management of Electronic Books.* Chicago: ALA.

Staenberg, Linda, and Susan Vanneman. 2013. How Special Is That Special Collection?" *School Library Monthly* 29 (5): 38–40.

Appendix B

Checklist for a Written Collection Development Plan

EXECUTIVE SUMMARY

- Does the summary focus on student learning?
- Is the summary one page or less?
- Is the summary accessible to all stakeholders (i.e. free of jargon, clear and to the point)?
- Does the summary provide an overview of the anticipated budget?

GUIDING STATEMENTS

- Does the school or school district have a mission statement that will guide this collection development plan?
- Does the library have a mission statement that is linked to the school or school district's mission statement and reflects the mission statement from AASL's *Empowering Learners: Guidelines for School Library Programs* (See Appendix F)?

- What does the School Board Selection Policy say about the selection of library materials?
- How do the Library Bill of Rights, the Interpretation for School Libraries, or other AASL position statements support the school library's selection of materials?
- Which selection criteria and tools will guide selection decisions?
- What goals for the school library's collection will support the goals of the school and/or school district's improvement plans?

NEEDS ASSESSMENT

- Does the needs assessment include information about the student demographics, learning needs, and student interests?
- Does the needs assessment address the neighborhood and community?
- Does the needs assessment include student achievement data?
- Does the needs assessment include data from individual fill rates, student surveys, or other measures of student interests and needs?
- Does the needs assessment include student access to technology, devices, or infrastructure needed to access materials in all formats?
- Does the needs assessment include data from collection mapping or output measures, such as the curriculum support rate, to demonstrate support of student learning standards?
- Are there gaps in the collection related to these standards?
- Are there particular standards that are not currently supported with sufficient, up-to-date library materials?
- Are there areas of the collection that are outdated or worn out?
- Does the assessment of the collection include all formats, including print, electronic, and equipment needs?

LONG-RANGE AND SHORT-TERM GOALS

- Do long-range goals for the next 3-5 years address areas of concern identified in the needs assessment?
- Do long-range goals address the entire collection?

- Do long-range goals clearly address student learning?
- Do long-range goals include an implementation timeline?
- Are there short-term acquisition goals (for the upcoming academic year) that address areas of concern?
- Are short-term goals realistic, attainable, and measurable?
- Do long-range and short-term goals include plans for weeding sections identified in the needs assessment?

BUDGET

- Are there budget estimates for each of the long-range goals?
- Is there a detailed budget to meet the short-term goals?
- Does the detailed budget include:
  - a variety of formats including print and electronic materials?
  - estimates based on actual current costs?
  - likely vendors or suppliers?
  - processing, handling, or shipping fees?
  - equipment, storage, devices, peripherals, or infrastructure?
  - recurring costs such as subscriptions or licenses?
  - a timeline for submitting orders?
- Do long-range goals address likely replacements, repairs, and recurring costs of subscriptions and licenses?
- Are there priorities for purchases that may be addressed as additional funds are procured through grants, community partners, or other sources?

PLAN FOR PROMOTION & CONTINUOUS EVALUATION

- Is there a plan for publicizing new acquisitions to students, staff, and community?
- Is there a plan for any training needed for new formats or equipment?
- Is there a plan for continuing needs assessments including output measures?

Recommended Selection Aids

JOURNALS WITH REVIEWS

Booklist (books) <www.booklistonline.com>

School Library Journal (books and other media) <www.slj.com>

LMC: Library Media Connection (books and other media) <www.librarymediaconnection.com>

Teacher Librarian (books and other media) <www.teacherlibrarian.com>

Horn Book Magazine (books) <www.hbook.com>

Kirkus Reviews (books) <www.kirkusreviews.com>

VOYA: Voice of Youth Advocates (books and other media) <www.voyamagazine.com>

CORE COLLECTIONS (FOR BOOKS AND MAGAZINES)

The H.W. Wilson "Core Collection" titles are available in hardcopy from Grey House Publishing <www.hwwilsoninprint.com/core_collections.

php>. Online access is available through EBSCO Host <www.ebscohost.com/academic/core-collections>.

Children's Core Collection
Middle & Junior High Core Collection
Senior High Core Collection

AWARDS AND BEST OF LISTS

American Association of School Librarians (AASL) Best Lists

Best Apps for Teaching & Learning <www.ala.org/aasl/standards-guidelines/best-apps>

Best Websites for Teaching & Learning <www.ala.org/aasl/standards-guidelines/best-websites>

These lists recognize and honor websites and apps of exceptional value to inquiry-based teaching and learning as embodied in AASL's *Standards for the 21st-Century Learner*. Listed resources foster the qualities of innovation, creativity, active participation, and collaboration. The tools are user-friendly and, therefore, encourage a community of learners to explore and discover.

American Library Association (ALA) Youth Awards and Lists

Association for Library Services to Children (ALSC) Book and Media Awards <www.ala.org/alsc/awardsgrants/bookmedia>

ALSC administers numerous awards for materials for youth (birth through fourteen years) including the prestigious Newbery and Caldecott awards. The awards, their criteria, and lists of winners can be accessed from this webpage.

Association for Library Services to Children (ALSC) Notable Lists <www.ala.org/alsc/awardsgrants/notalists>

In addition to the awards, several ALSC committees compile annual lists of notable books, audio recordings, and videos. Links to these lists can be found on this webpage.

Young Adult Library Services Association (YALSA) Book Awards and Book/
Media Lists <www.ala.org/yalsa/bookawards/booklists/members>

> YALSA administers several awards, including Printz and Morris, and
> numerous lists of the best books, graphic novels, films, and audio-
> books for teens ages twelve through eighteen.

Association of American University Presses (AAUP)

University Press Books for Public and Secondary School Libraries <www.
aaupnet.org/librarybooks>

> This is an annual collection-development tool published with the
> help of two divisions of ALA: the American Association of School
> Librarians (AASL) and the Collection Development and Evalua-
> tion Section of the Reference and User Services Association (RUSA/
> CODES). Print copies of the bibliography are available to librarians
> free of charge. A link to the order form is on the page at the URL
> above.

Appendix D
Publications from AASL

American Association of School Librarians offers a rich variety of publications on topics essential to school librarians everywhere. To read descriptions of each publication and to order, go to <www.ala.org/aasl/booksproducts>. Order online at <www.alastore.ala.org/aasl>.

LEARNING STANDARDS AND PROGRAM GUIDELINES

Standards for the 21st-Century Learner (2007)
Available for free download (PDF) at <www.ala.org/aasl/standards>. Packets of full-color brochures may also be purchased.

Standards for the 21st-Century Learner in Action (2009)

Empowering Learners: Guidelines for School Library Programs (2009)

A Planning Guide for Empowering Learners with School Library Program Assessment Rubric (2010)

> Available for purchase at <www.aasl.eb.com>, or for more information and resources visit <www.ala.org/aasl/planningguide>.

A 21st-Century Approach to School Librarian Evaluation (2012)

Library Spaces for 21st-Century Learners: A Planning Guide for Creating New School Library Concepts (2013) **NEW!**

Empowering Leadership: Developing Behaviors for Success (2013) **NEW!**

Developing Collections to Empower Learners (2014) **NEW!**

OTHER AASL PUBLICATIONS

Assessing Student Learning in the School Library Media Center (2007)

Best of *Knowledge Quest* series:

> *Instructional Partnerships: A Pathway to Leadership* (2013) **NEW!**
>
> *School Library Media Programs in Action: Civic Engagement, Social Justice, and Equity* (2009)
>
> *School Library Services in a Multicultural Society* (2009)

Collection Development for the School Library Media Program (2006)

Ebooks and the School Library Program: A Practical Guide for the School Librarian (2013) **NEW!**

Every Student Reads: Collaboration and Reading to Learn (2005)

The Power of Data: An Introduction to Using Local, State, and National Data to Support School Library Programs (2012)

ADVOCACY TOOLS

School Library Programs Create Lifelong Learners: A Student's and Parent's Guide to Evaluating Independent School Libraries (2011)

Advocacy Brochure Series: *School Library Programs Improve Student Learning* (2011)

> Available for free download (PDF) at <www.ala.org/aasl/advocacy-brochures>. Packets of full-color brochures may also be purchased.

Appendix E

AASL Position Statement on Quantitative Standards

Quantitative standards offer baseline numbers for everything from budgets to numbers of periodical subscriptions to square feet of shelving space. They provide a measure that allows comparisons for individual school libraries as well as a means to advocate for new resources. Minimal standards, however, are problematic because they can also be considered sufficient, or even "ideal," with the unintended consequence of providing a ceiling rather than a floor for evaluating a school library program and justifying new resources. Quantitative standards are also difficult to establish because they require continuous updating to represent new formats and new technologies. More significantly, quantitative measures are silent about quality. Any measure of the school library's resources or program requires interpretation and application by a trained school library professional working collaboratively with the school library's stakeholders to define and evaluate a high-quality school library program.

In the history of school libraries, national quantitative standards provided guidance for the minimal size of collections, space needed for facilities, and adequate staffing. These standards led to significant growth in early school libraries and offered baseline numbers for the allocation of school funding. They were ultimately about access: sufficient quantities of resources, time, and space for students and staff in a building to have sufficient access to the high quality and current materials needed for reading and learning. As we move toward a future where technology is essentially ubiquitous, the standards needed for access are of an entirely different order from those of the Twentieth Century. Many of today's students have unprecedented access to unlimited quantities of information; access issues in this context are about selected quality not quantity. Issues of equity also persist and are exacerbated by technological gaps. These kinds of access issues vary from locality to locality and with the introduction of new technologies.

School librarians should engage in a continuous evaluation of the effectiveness of the school library program to meet the needs of patrons for access to ideas and information through the resources of the library. Such an evaluation should be locally based, responsive to community needs, and flexible to allow for new formats, new modes of access, and changing demographics. National attempts to provide quantitative measures would lose this local context and flexibility. Rather than quantitative standards that promote compliance with an inflexible and minimal list, school librarians need the dispositions of deep commitment and inquiry required by continuous program assessment and advocacy with stakeholders.

AASL offers several tools for program evaluation:

- The *Position Statement on Appropriate Staffing for School Libraries* could be of help in thinking through access issues as well as supervisory functions of school library personnel, both laterally and within the school district structure. <http://www.ala.org/aasl/aaslissues/positionstatements/appropriatestaffing>

- *Essential Links: Resources for School Library Program Development* provides guidelines for collection development by school level. <http://essentiallinks.aasl.org>

- *School Libraries Count!* provides national statistics including collection size and per pupil expenditures that may be used as a benchmark for local school libraries. Several states compile similar statistics and reports. <http://www.ala.org/aasl/research/slc>

- *A Planning Guide for Empowering Learners* offers a structure for evaluating and envisioning an exemplary school library program. <http://www.ala.org/aasl/standards-guidelines/planning-guide>

As new technologies develop and new formats emerge, school librarians remain committed to providing students with access to high-quality and up-to-date resources for learning.

Adopted 06/28/13

Source: http://www.ala.org/aasl/advocacy/resources/position-statements/ quantitative

Appendix F

Extended Mission Statement from *Empowering Learners*

In 2009 AASL revised the mission of the school library program to reflect the expanding responsibilities of the school librarian in helping learners develop the skills needed to be successful in work and in life in the twenty-first century. The revised mission statement appears below:

The mission of the school library program is to ensure that students and staff are effective users of ideas and information. The school librarian empowers students to be critical thinkers, enthusiastic readers, skillful researchers, and ethical users of information by:

- collaborating with educators and students to design and teach engaging learning experiences that meet individual needs.

- instructing students and assisting educators in using, evaluating, and producing information and ideas through active use of a broad range of appropriate tools, resources, and information technologies.

- providing access to materials in all formats, including up-to-date, high- quality, varied literature to develop and strengthen a love of reading.
- providing students and staff with instruction and resources that reflect current information needs and anticipate changes in technology and education.
- providing leadership in the total education program and advocating for strong school library programs as essential to meeting local, state, and national education goals.

Source: *Empowering Learners: Guidelines for School Library Programs* (AASL 2009, 8)

Appendix G

Learning4Life (L4L)

A National Plan for Implementation of
Standards for the 21st-Century Learner
and *Empowering Learners: Guidelines
for School Library Programs*

An initiative of the American Association of School Librarians

This implementation plan was created to support states, school systems, and individual schools preparing to implement AASL's *Standards for the 21st-Century Learner* and *Empowering Learners: Guidelines for School Library Programs*. The plan will also increase awareness and understanding of the learning standards and program guidelines, and create a committed group of stakeholders with a shared voice.

While the standards and guidelines define what "should be" in terms of information literacy, research through guided inquiry, and integration of technology in the traditional school context, they also acknowledge varied and new forms of teaching and learning in a social and global context.

Foundational to this plan is the fundamental value of reading, core content, and mastery of skills that produce deep knowledge and understanding, as well as the portable skills that serve individuals for a lifetime, making them critical thinkers, problem solvers, and continually evolving learners.

To this end, the L4L implementation plan addresses the practical realization of these important skills and values as it:

- identifies guiding principles and an overarching position and branding statement;
- identifies target audiences (internal and external);
- identifies training opportunities and resources;
- provides a communication plan;
- provides a plan for continuous feedback, evaluation, and sustainability;
- provides a plan for endorsements and support; and
- provides supporting documents.

The plan is available online at <www.ala.org/aasl/learning4life>.

Interlocking Pieces Graphic designed
by Louis Henry Mitchell

Appendix H
Index

standards

    curriculum, viii, ix, 15, 21, 23, 30, 52, *see also* Common Core State Standards

    information literacy, 72

    library, 2, 71

students with disabilities, *see* disabilities

subscriptions, 69

survey, 30, 73, 74, 81, 87

T

textbooks, 24, 39, 49, 65

tools, 5, 28-9, 52-56, 81

V

vendors, 17, 35, 54, 62

volunteers, 74, 78

W

web resources, 39-40

weeding, vii, 17, 61, 73, 82

Winkel, Lois, 96

Wired Magazine, 61

wish lists, 90

Appendix I

Tables and Figures

TABLES

FIGURES